# TRADING AND ELECTRONIC MARKETS: WHAT INVESTMENT PROFESSIONALS NEED TO KNOW

Larry Harris, CFA

CFA Institute
Research
Foundation

## Statement of Purpose

The CFA Institute Research Foundation is a not-for-profit organization established to promote the development and dissemination of relevant research for investment practitioners worldwide.

Cover Image Photo Credit: iStock.com/Maxiphoto

ISBN 978-1-934667-91-0

19 October 2015

### Editorial Staff

Stephen Smith
Editor

Cindy Maisannes
*Manager*, Publications Production

Pat Light
Assistant Editor

Mike Dean
Publishing Technology Specialist

SUSTAINABLE FORESTRY INITIATIVE
Certified Sourcing
www.sfiprogram.org
SFI-01681

# Biography

**Larry Harris, CFA,** holds the Fred V. Keenan Chair in Finance at the University of Southern California Marshall School of Business. He has written extensively about trading rules, transaction costs, and market regulations, including an introduction to the economics of trading, *Trading and Exchanges: Market Microstructure for Practitioners.* Professor Harris served as chief economist of the SEC and contributed extensively to the development of regulations implemented in the Sarbanes–Oxley Act, the resolution of the mutual fund timing crisis, the specification of Regulation NMS (National Market System), the promotion of bond price transparency, and numerous legal cases. He also directed the SEC Office of Economic Analysis. Professor Harris currently serves as lead independent director of Interactive Brokers, Inc. (IBKR), director of the Selected Funds, and research coordinator for the Institute for Quantitative Research in Finance (the Q-Group). He is a former director of CFA Society Los Angeles and a former associate editor of the *Journal of Finance*, the *Review of Financial Studies*, and the *Journal of Financial and Quantitative Analysis*. Professor Harris holds a PhD in economics from the University of Chicago.

# Contents

# Foreword

No aspect of investment management has undergone more radical change in the past decade than trading. With the proliferation of electronic trading, new intermediaries, new securities, a new regulatory regime, dark pools, and the need for speed, the already arcane world of market microstructure has entered a new realm of uncharted territory. And no one is more qualified to decipher this complex new world than Larry Harris.

Harris begins with a discussion of trading as a zero-sum game before transaction costs and a negative-sum game after transaction costs, and he describes what this implies for informed and uninformed traders. He goes on to describe why people trade, distinguishing those who seek to profit from those who are motivated by utilitarian needs, such as the demand for liquidity. He introduces a taxonomy in which speculators fall into two groups: informed traders who rely on information about fundamental value and parasitic traders who seek to anticipate the trading patterns of other traders. He describes several strategies of parasitic traders, pointing out that some strategies are illegal while others, though legal, are unethical. Harris also discusses liquidity providers, including dealers who enable their clients to trade when they want to and arbitrageurs who connect buyers and sellers in different markets with the goal of profiting from pricing discrepancies.

Harris then introduces the notion of adverse selection and describes how it enables informed traders to profit from uninformed traders. He next addresses transaction costs and presents several methods for estimating them. He also points out how important it is for portfolio managers to explain their trading motivation to traders and for traders to convey information about current market conditions to portfolio managers.

Harris next tackles the new world of electronic trading. He describes automated order creation and submission systems and discusses why these electronic systems lower transaction costs and how they provide several other benefits to the markets. Harris confronts the fact that electronic trading offers advantages to parasitic traders, but he argues that the resultant reduction in transaction costs more than offsets the ill effects of parasitic trading. He also addresses the more fundamental issue of whether high-speed trading advances the cause of capital formation.

Harris concludes with a discussion of practitioner and regulatory issues, in which he examines the potential increase in systemic risk brought on by high-speed trading as well as the adverse impact of dark pools on price discovery. Thankfully, he offers several recommendations for addressing these new risks. As a bonus, Harris includes an appendix in which he provides a forensic analysis of the Flash Crash.

The content of this book is complex, but Harris presents it in a style that is concise and lucid yet never superficial. His economy of words is admirable. I cannot think of a more efficient way to learn the key elements of today's market microstructure than to read this excellent exposition. And even if trading is not central to the way you participate in the markets, I cannot think of a more productive way to spend a couple of hours! There is something in Larry Harris's excellent book for everyone, and the CFA Institute Research Foundation is uncommonly pleased to present it.

Mark P. Kritzman, CFA
CEO, Windham Capital Management
September 2015

# 1. Introduction

The solutions to many financial problems involve trading in organized markets. Consider some examples:

- Investors buy securities to move money from the present to the future.

- Borrowers sell bonds to move money from the future to the present.

- Hedgers buy and sell various derivative contracts to manage their net exposure to risks that concern them.

- Various entities buy and sell currencies to ensure that they can make payments throughout the world.

Solving these problems successfully requires that traders effectively execute orders while appropriately controlling their transaction costs. This book provides buy-side financial analysts, investment managers, and investment sponsors with the tools to understand and manage recent innovations in trading that involve the automation of both trading systems and trading strategies. Mastery of the concepts presented here will allow financial managers to better manage their investment and trading strategies.

My presentation assumes that readers have a basic understanding of order types and of the organization of order-driven exchanges. Those who are completely unfamiliar with these topics will be able to follow most of the discussion, but they may occasionally need to look up some definitions.

Much of this book is about liquidity—the ability to trade when and where you want to trade, in significant size and without much cost. We will discuss the traders who *supply liquidity* to the market—they offer other traders opportunities to trade. And we will discuss the traders who take these opportunities—they *demand liquidity*. Synonyms for supplying liquidity include offering liquidity, making markets, and posting liquidity. Synonyms for demanding liquidity include taking liquidity and hitting the market.

The first two chapters of this book are of general interest to all financial analysts, investment managers, and investment sponsors. They explain why people trade and how traders win and lose in the markets. The concepts presented are essential for understanding electronic trading issues, but they have a much more fundamental value: They provide the theoretical underpinning for understanding when active investment management will be successful.

Chapter 2 presents a taxonomy of why people trade. Some readers may be tempted to skip this chapter, thinking that they already have a good handle on why people trade. I strongly discourage them from doing so. The failures of investment managers to understand why they trade, and why others trade, explain most of the mistakes that investment managers make. *Investment discipline* ultimately is all about trading only when you rationally expect to achieve your trading objectives. It thus follows that those who do not clearly understand why they and others trade will lack the investment discipline needed to perform well. You will find that the organization of this taxonomy makes it easy to understand why markets exist, who makes them liquid, how information gets into prices, when informed traders profit, and how some traders exploit other traders.

The next chapter examines the implications of the zero-sum game for investment management. Trading is a zero-sum game when gains and losses are measured relative to the market index. Traders must fully understand the implications of this vital accounting identity to form rational expectations of when they can expect to achieve their investment objectives—and at what cost. In my experience, conscious appreciation of this identity and its implications is the single marker that most clearly distinguishes successful investment managers (and their sponsors) from mediocre ones.

Chapter 4 considers how and why investment managers and their sponsors measure and control transaction costs. Good transaction cost analyses also provide managers with essential information about what their competitors are doing, thus enabling them to form expectations about whether their trading will be successful.

The book turns to electronic trading in Chapter 5, which identifies the factors that led to the adoption of electronic trading systems and to the implementation of electronic trading strategies. This discussion explains why speed is so important to electronic traders and how they obtain it.

Chapter 6 examines practitioner and regulatory issues associated with electronic trading. The discussion covers nine major issues, ranging from whether the economy really benefits from so much speed to rule changes that would produce better markets for buy-side traders.

I conclude the main text with a brief note about electronic trading in bond markets. A short appendix explains what happened during the 2010 Flash Crash and identifies its causes.

The remainder of this chapter explains why understanding trading and the zero-sum game is so important to investment managers.

## 1.1. Importance to Investment Managers

Investing is a zero-sum game when performance is measured relative to the value-weighted market index. The aggregate gains of all investors who beat the market are exactly equal to the aggregate losses of all investors who underperform the market. This equality follows from the fact that all securities are owned by someone. Accordingly, the average return to holding all securities in the market (the return to the value-weighted market index) must equal the value-weighted return of all investment portfolios formed from those securities. If some investors beat the market, others must underperform.

Because investors incur transaction costs when they trade, investing—especially active investing—is a negative-sum game. Controlling transaction costs thus is essential for investors who seek to beat the market. Of course, all traders who want to preserve or grow their capital must control transaction costs, regardless of how they benchmark their performance.

Investment managers concerned about beating their peers should consider the following fact: Among large blend equity mutual funds, only 87 bps separate the return performance of the 40th percentile fund from that of the 60th percentile fund in the distribution of annualized total five-year returns.[1] Poor traders can lose that much in transaction costs during the course of a year, especially if they trade frequently.

## 1.2. Why Uninformed Traders Underperform

The observation that trading is a zero-sum game (or a negative-sum game when transaction costs are included) has an extremely important implication for active investment managers who base their trading decisions on financial analyses. Those managers who regularly underperform the market do not do so because they systematically choose the wrong securities to hold in their portfolios. Such managers could easily adjust their trading strategies to simply do the opposite of whatever their analyses suggest and thereby beat the market. The financial analyses of underperforming managers thus are not systematically wrong.[2] Instead, they are systematically uninformative—sometimes they are right and sometimes they are wrong.

---

[1]This calculation is based on my analysis of five-year annual returns reported by Morningstar as of 2 January 2015 (news.morningstar.com/fund-category-returns/large-blend/$FOCA$LB. aspx).

[2]This conclusion assumes that all managers evaluate their performance and adjust accordingly. Some behavioral biases may suggest otherwise. For example, risk aversion and herding may cause some managers to systematically sell when the market is undervalued and to buy when the market is overvalued.

One would think that such managers obtain the market return on average since they presumably buy winning securities and losing securities with equal probabilities over time. This conclusion would be correct if they could always trade without cost. Unfortunately for them (and all other traders), trading is costly. Investment managers who base their trading decisions on poor financial analyses lose on average simply because they trade. They could avoid these losses if they held the market index portfolio.

Now consider the active investment managers who regularly beat the market. Their financial analyses somehow predict which securities will rise and which will fall with greater precision than they could obtain by simply flipping a coin. These managers buy securities that they expect will rise and they sell those that they expect will fall. On average, the securities that they expect will rise do rise, and those that they expect will fall do fall. They profit if their average trading profits are greater than their transaction costs.

These active managers beat the market because they can trade on the right side of the market. Note that they cannot profit if they cannot trade.

Where do their profits come from? Because trading is a zero-sum game, they must come from other traders. But if the other traders are systematically neither right nor wrong on average, the profits cannot be due to poor security selection decisions made by the other investors. Instead, those investment managers who win on average must somehow profit simply from the fact that others are willing to trade with them.

This conclusion, which is extremely important to understanding the determinants of successful active investment management, bears repeating: *Active investment managers can profit only if other traders are willing to trade with them.* Even well-informed traders whose forecasts about future prices are mostly correct can profit from their superior vision only if others are willing to trade with them.

# 2.   A Taxonomy of Why People Trade

Understanding why people trade is essential to understanding all trading issues involving market structure, regulation, and trading strategies. This chapter provides a brief taxonomy of why people trade. The classification of traders is important because it helps make clear who loses and who wins when trading—and why. This taxonomy is particularly important for financial analysts who estimate fundamental values and changes in fundamental values because it identifies when their analyses are likely to produce profits. It also provides the foundation for understanding many strategies used by electronic traders.

People trade for many different reasons, and more than one reason may contribute to the decision to arrange a given trade. For example, investors who need to move money from the present to the future also may try to speculate by picking securities that they believe will outperform the market. For simplicity, the discussion in this chapter separately considers the reasons why people trade as though only one reason motivates every trade.

In practice, the decision to trade is often quite complex. That complexity ensures that many investors and risk managers—including many financial professionals—often do not recognize all the factors that influence their decisions to trade. When some factors do not promote their investment and risk management mandates, managers may make poor trading decisions. Understanding why people trade thus is essential for managers who seek to maintain effective investment discipline. Breaking these reasons down into simple building blocks is the best way to understand them.

This point bears repeating: *Understanding the reasons why people trade can help investment managers and risk managers improve their discipline.* The most successful managers trade only when they expect that trading will advance their mission. Achieving that discipline requires managers to understand exactly why they are trading and to recognize when they may be tempted to trade for other reasons.

The discussion starts by distinguishing between proprietary traders and agency traders. It then distinguishes between those traders whose primary purpose for trading is utilitarian and those whose primary purpose is to produce trading profits. The bulk of this chapter introduces the three main types of proprietary traders—informed traders, parasitic traders, and liquidity suppliers—and their various trading strategies.

## 2.1. The Taxonomy

The first distinction among traders is between *proprietary traders*, who trade for their own accounts, and *agency traders*, who trade for other account holders. Brokers and buy-side traders are agents who serve other traders. Although brokers and buy-side traders often engage in similar activities, they differ in how many clients they serve and in how their clients compensate them. *Brokers* typically work for brokerage firms that serve many clients, and their clients usually compensate them (or their firms) with commissions on the trades that they arrange. In contrast, *buy-side traders* typically work for one client—their employer, usually an investment management firm that may employ many portfolio managers—and they are compensated with salary and bonuses. Brokers and buy-side traders generally just arrange trades that their clients or employers request.

In contrast, proprietary traders decide what and how much they want to trade. They may trade for their own accounts, or they may trade as agents for clients for whom they may manage investments, risk exposures, or cash flows.

The most important distinction among proprietary traders concerns why they participate in the markets. *Profit-motivated traders* trade only because they want to obtain trading profits. For example, dealers, arbitrageurs, and speculators trade because they expect to buy at prices lower than those at which they sell and thereby profit from their trading.

In contrast, *utilitarian traders* trade because they use the markets to obtain benefits that are unrelated to trading profits. Consider some examples:

- *Investors* trade securities to move money from the present to the future, whereas *borrowers* trade to move money from the future to the present. These traders solve intertemporal cash flow problems—they have money at one point in time but they need it at another point in time.

- *Hedgers* trade contracts to transfer to other traders risks that they are uncomfortable holding. These traders often use futures contracts or insurance contracts to divest risk.

- *Companies* trade foreign exchange so they can make payments in required currencies. These traders exchange assets that are of lesser value to them for assets that are of greater value.

- *Gamblers* trade to obtain risk exposures that may excite them, entertain them, or allow them to amuse others with their stories. These traders may include people whose hobby is trading and many others who trade in part because they enjoy trading, whether they recognize it or not. Although the term gambler often has a pejorative connotation, in this context it simply refers to traders who derive some form of pleasure from trading.

In all these cases, utilitarian traders—like all traders—hope to profit by buying low and selling high. In contrast to profit-motivated traders, however, trading profits do not ultimately motivate their trades. Rather, utilitarians trade because the markets provide them with services that they cannot obtain as easily or as cheaply elsewhere.

Note that utilitarian traders are willing to incur transaction costs so they can obtain their intended utilitarian benefits from trading. Their willingness to pay to use the markets is the ultimate source of the profits earned by profit-motivated traders.

Profit-motivated traders include speculators and liquidity suppliers. Speculators trade on information about future prices. They buy when they expect prices to rise and sell when they expect prices to fall. In contrast, liquidity suppliers trade to help connect buyers with sellers who are not at the same place at the same time. In particular, *dealers* connect buyers with sellers who arrive at different times in a given market, whereas *arbitrageurs* connect buyers with sellers who arrive at the same time in different markets.

Speculators differ by the types of information they use to predict future prices. *Informed traders* trade on information about the fundamental values of securities and contracts. In contrast, *parasitic traders* trade on information about the trades that they expect other traders will want to do.[3]

## 2.2.　Informed Traders: Value Traders and News Traders

Informed traders include those who estimate fundamental values and those who estimate changes in fundamental values. The former are called value traders and the latter are called news traders.[4] The distinction is important because they operate quite differently and have very different impacts on the markets.

*Value traders* estimate fundamental values of securities and contracts. *Fundamental value* is the value that all traders would agree to if all traders knew all available information about the instrument and if they all agreed on the implications of that information. (Fundamental value is also called intrinsic or "true" value.) Equity and fixed-income analysts often try to estimate fundamental values, which, of course, nobody ever observes. Value traders buy those

---

[3]For those readers who are paying attention to my writing, please accept my apologies for using the root word "trade" four times in this sentence. For those who are not, be assured that this note is the only such comment you will find.

[4]In discussions about market microstructure, the term "value trader" refers to entities that estimate security and contract values as opposed to those who confine their trading to value stocks in contrast to growth stocks.

　　**7**

securities and contracts that they believe are undervalued in the market and sell those that they believe are overvalued. They profit if market prices move toward their value estimates. The best value traders are excellent financial analysts who have superb access to current information about finances, technologies, product and input markets, the macroeconomy, and interest rates.

*News traders* trade when they believe that new information about changes in fundamental values has not yet caused prices to change. To trade successfully, they must obtain new information before other traders, that information must have material implications for valuations, and prices cannot already have changed to reflect the news. Unlike value traders, news traders need not know the fundamental values of the instruments that they trade. They simply must know how news events cause those values to change. The best news traders collect, recognize, and act on material information before other traders.

**When Informed Traders Profit.** Note that informed traders can profit only when price is different from fundamental value. If prices generally are close to fundamental values, as we would expect them to be in efficient markets, informed traders can profit only when prices change and fundamental values do not or when fundamental values change and prices do not.

The first case—prices change but fundamental values do not—can occur only when uninformed traders cause prices to change. The value traders will profit because they estimate fundamental values and can recognize when prices do not reflect fundamental values. Note that value traders thus supply liquidity—at least indirectly—to the uninformed traders, who cause prices to change. For example, if uninformed traders push prices down, value traders will eventually buy, which will cause prices to rise.

The second case—prices do not change but fundamental values do— occurs when events cause fundamental values to change. News traders generally are the first to learn about such events.

Value traders and news traders thus can be distinguished by the events that produce their profitable trading opportunities. For value traders, those events are the price impacts of uninformed traders. In contrast, news traders trade on events that cause fundamental values to change.

**Informative Prices and Informed Trading Profits.** The trading of speculators and news traders generally causes prices to reflect the information on which they base their trading decisions. In particular, when they buy, they tend to push up the prices of securities that they believe are undervalued. Likewise, when they sell, they tend to decrease the prices of securities that they believe are overvalued. If their beliefs are well founded—that is, if they have correctly interpreted their information—their trading will cause prices to more closely reflect fundamental values. If so, analysts say that prices reflect the traders' information.

Informed trading is profitable when the profits that informed traders make from trading exceed the costs of acquiring and processing the information on which they make their trading decisions. Their trading profits depend on their costs of trading. In particular, if they cannot establish significant positions in their securities without moving prices substantially, they will be unable to profit much from their trading. Informed trading thus is more profitable in liquid markets. The trading profits of informed traders also depend on the materiality of their information. Informed traders profit more when they can correctly identify that prices are very different from fundamental values than when their research identifies only small differences.

The competition among informed traders seeking trading profits causes prices to be more informative. As prices become more informative, the opportunities for further speculative trading profits decrease.

If too many informed traders are in the markets, not all of them may be able to cover the costs of acquiring, processing, and acting on information because the pool of liquidity available to them is finite. (This pool ultimately depends on the willingness of utilitarian traders to trade.) Those whose trades are unprofitable will eventually quit if they trade only in pursuit of profits. Their withdrawal from the markets will increase the profits of the remaining informed traders as their share of the total available liquidity increases. In contrast, if trading on information is quite profitable, word generally gets around and new informed traders will enter the markets to compete for those profits. Their entry will lower everyone's profits as they demand a share of the available liquidity.

These arguments suggest that the number of informed traders depends on the costs of acquiring and processing information and on the total liquidity available to informed traders. In particular, informed traders will exit when informed trading is insufficiently profitable and they will enter when it is excessively profitable. In equilibrium—when no entry or exit occurs—informed trading for the least efficient traders will be just profitable enough to cover their costs of acquiring and processing the information on which they make their trading decisions.

Prices can never fully incorporate all available information. Informed traders will not invest in information that is costly to acquire if they do not expect that its implications for values will be sufficiently material to allow them to generate the trading profits necessary to cover their information costs. This statement has two implications for how informative prices will be and thus for better understanding the efficient market hypothesis. Prices will be most informative for instruments (1) that trade in liquid markets and (2) whose fundamental values analysts can easily estimate. Liquid markets are necessary to allow informed traders to profit. Low information costs are necessary to ensure that informed traders acquire and act on all material information. Many countries and exchanges have rules that mandate financial disclosures to lower the costs of acquiring information and thereby make prices more informative.

## 2.3. Parasitic Traders

Parasitic traders are speculators who base their predictions about future prices on information they obtain about orders that other traders intend, or will soon intend, to fill. Parasitic traders include front runners, who trade in front of traders who demand liquidity; quote matchers, who trade in front of traders who supply liquidity; sentiment-oriented technical traders, who anticipate the orders that uninformed traders intend to fill; and market manipulators, who fool or force others into making disadvantageous trades.

**Front Runners.** *Front runners* are parasitic traders who know or infer the trades that other traders intend to actively arrange by demanding liquidity. They know that traders who demand liquidity cause prices to rise when buying and fall when selling. Accordingly, they buy in front of anticipated purchases, and they sell in front of anticipated sales. In most jurisdictions, front running is illegal if the front runners acquire their information about orders improperly—for example, by a tip from a broker handling a large order.

Some traders use electronic artificial intelligence systems to identify when traders are filling large orders over time by breaking them up into small pieces. When these traders suspect that buyers or sellers are working large orders, they will trade ahead on the same side with the hope of benefiting when the large traders move prices as they fill their orders. This front-running strategy is legal if the information on which it is based is properly obtained— for example, by watching a market data feed.

Front running increases transaction costs for the traders whose orders are front-run, because the front runners take liquidity that the front-run traders otherwise would have taken for themselves.

**Quote Matchers.** *Quote matchers* are parasitic traders who exploit the option values of standing limit orders. A standing limit sell order is a call option granted to the market as a whole, because it gives anyone willing to buy at the limit price an option to trade. Likewise, a standing limit buy order is a put option. The options provided by standing orders are available only to the first traders to take them. They disappear when other traders take them or when the limit traders cancel them.

All options have value. Although the options inherent in orders cannot be bought or sold, fast (and clever) traders can often exploit their values through the quote-matching trading strategy, which is best described with an example.

Suppose that a large trader places an exposed limit order to buy at 20. A clever trader—the quote matcher—then tries to buy at the lowest possible price. Depending on the market structure, the quote matcher may be able to buy at 20 in another market, or time precedence rules (that give the first order at a given price precedence over all other orders) may force the quote matcher to buy at a slightly improved (higher) price (e.g., 20.01).

Following the quote matcher's purchase, the quote matcher has a valuable position in the market: If the price rises, the quote matcher will profit from the price rise. But if the quote matcher believes that prices will fall—perhaps because the quote matcher sees that the prices of correlated securities are dropping—the quote matcher will sell to the large limit order buyer and thereby bound the quote matcher's losses.

Quote matchers hurt standing limit order traders who might have traded had the quote matchers not traded in front of their orders. In this example, if the price rises, the limit order buyer loses the opportunity to profit. If the price falls, the limit order buyer loses.

The quote-matching strategy works best when quote matchers can act faster than traders who submit limit orders. Accordingly, only electronic traders can execute the strategy profitably.

**Sentiment-Oriented Technical Traders.** The trading of certain uninformed traders is often predictable. Consider two examples:

- Many traders sell when prices fall and buy when prices rise. They often sell because they fear greater losses, and they often buy when they mistakenly believe that past performance predicts future performance or when they envy the gains made by others.

- Many traders often respond to the same information signals. If that information is already in the price, practitioners say that they are trading on *stale information*. Though such traders think they are informed traders, they are not; they are just late to the game. Some observant traders can predict when other traders will trade on stale information—for example, after important announcements that merely confirm information that many other traders already knew or had easily predicted and that thus was already in the price.

**11**

Traders who can identify these behavioral biases may profit by anticipating the orders from traders subject to these biases. Such traders are *technical traders* because they typically base their trades on market information rather than on fundamental information. They are *sentiment-oriented technical traders* because they try to identify the sentiment (direction) of other traders.

**Market Manipulators.** *Market manipulators* are parasitic traders who speculate on future price changes that they attempt to control. They profit from trades that they fool or force other traders into doing. In general, market manipulation consists of any trading strategy whose purpose is to produce misleading or false market prices, quotes, or fundamental information in an attempt to profit from distorting the normal operation of markets. Many market manipulation strategies exist—including bluffing, squeezing, cornering, and gunning—all of which are discussed later in this section.

In most jurisdictions, market manipulation strategies are illegal. Enforcement is often difficult, however, because the exact infractions are hard to define and because prosecutors generally must prove scienter (a legal term meaning intent or knowledge of wrongdoing), which can be difficult when defendants suggest alternative explanations for their behavior.

Market manipulation strategies may involve the use of improper market activities such as trading for market impact, rumormongering, wash trading, and spoofing.

- *Trading for market impact* involves trading for the purpose of raising or lowering prices. A market manipulator often is willing to incur substantial transaction costs to raise or lower the price of a security in an effort to influence other traders' perceptions of value.

- *Rumormongering* is the dissemination of false information about fundamental values or about other traders' trading intentions in an attempt to alter investors' value assessments. Financial analysts must be careful to ensure that they base their analyses on valid information and not on false information designed to fool them into making poor decisions. Note that although rumormongering is illegal in most jurisdictions, simply reporting one side of an issue is not illegal. Financial analysts, therefore, must also be careful to ensure that they base their analyses on balanced information and not on information that is true but selectively presented to them with the purpose of distorting their analyses.

- *Wash trading* consists of trades arranged among commonly controlled accounts to create the impression of market activity at a particular price. The purpose of wash trading is to fool investors into believing that a market is more liquid than it truly is and to thereby increase investors' confidence both in their ability to exit positions without substantial cost and in their assessments of security values. Manipulators can also achieve these purposes by falsely reporting trades that never occurred, which is essentially what happens when they arrange trades among commonly controlled accounts.

- *Spoofing*, also known as *layering*, is a trading practice in which traders place exposed standing limit orders to convey an impression to other traders that the market is more liquid than it is or to suggest to other traders that the security is under- or overvalued. For example, suppose that a spoofer wants to buy stock cheaply or quickly. The spoofer might place a hidden buy order in the market. The spoofer then places one or more exposed sell limit orders in the market to convey the impression that prices may soon fall. Seeing the spoofing sell orders, one or more traders may conclude that values may be lower than market prices suggest. On that basis, they may sell into the spoofer's buy order, enabling the spoofer to obtain a quick and possibly cheaper purchase than the spoofer otherwise would have obtained had the spoofer not placed the spoofing sell orders. Of course, immediately following the execution of the buy order, the spoofer will cancel the sell orders.

Spoofing is risky because the spoofing orders that spoofers submit might execute before their intended orders execute. Spoofers can manage this risk by keeping track of the orders in the limit order book ahead of their spoofing orders. If these orders fill before the spoofers' intended orders fill, spoofers will cancel their spoofing orders to prevent them from executing. To effectively manage these processes, spoofers need to use electronic systems to monitor trading and to ensure that they can quickly cancel their orders as soon as they no longer want them to stand.

Although spoofing appears to be an illegal manipulative strategy (e.g., the US Securities and Exchange Commission [SEC] and the US Commodity Futures Trading Commission [CFTC] consider it illegal), it does have one probative value: Spoofing may be the best strategy that a legitimate investor can use to combat parasitic quote matching. Suppose that whenever a buyer places a limit order to buy, a quote matcher steps in front of the order with a better-priced buy order. The buyer can combat this behavior by simultaneously placing a spoofing limit sell order and a hidden limit buy order. If the quote matcher tries to quote-match the exposed limit sell order by submitting a lower-priced sell order, the quote matcher may fill the investor's hidden buy order. If so, the investor would immediately cancel the spoofing sell order.

Market manipulators often use these improper market activities singly or in combination when they try to fool or force other traders into trades that will ultimately prove to be disadvantageous to them.

■ *Bluffing.* Bluffers submit orders and arrange trades to influence other traders' perceptions of value. They often prey on momentum traders, who buy when prices are rising and sell when prices are falling. For example, consider typical "pump-and-dump" schemes, in which bluffers buy stock to raise its price and thereby encourage momentum traders to buy. The bluffers then sell the stock to the momentum traders at higher prices. To further the scheme, bluffers may engage in rumormongering or wash trading. Note also that bluffers may time their purchases to immediately follow the release of valid positive information about the security and thereby fool traders into overvaluing the material significance of the new information.

In a pump-and-dump manipulation, the bluffer tries to raise prices. Similar manipulations can occur on the short side, though they are less common. In such manipulations, manipulators take short positions and then try to repurchase shares at lower prices. These manipulations are often called "short and distorts."

To avoid falling into these traps, financial analysts must ensure that they base their analyses on independent assessments of value. In particular, their analyses must have a proper foundation as required by Principle V.A.2 of the CFA Institute Code of Ethics and Standards of Professional Conduct.[5]

■ *Gunning the market.* Gunning the market is a strategy used by market manipulators to force traders to do disadvantageous trades. A manipulator generally guns the market by selling quickly to push prices down with the hope of triggering stop-loss sell orders.

For example, suppose that a market manipulator believes that traders have placed many stop-loss sell orders at 50. The manipulator may sell aggressively to push prices down from 51 to 50 and thereby trigger the stop-loss sell orders. The manipulator may then be able to profit by repurchasing at lower prices.

■ *Squeezing and cornering.* Squeezing, cornering, and gunning the market are all schemes that market manipulators use to force traders to do disadvantageous trades. In a squeeze or corner, the manipulator surreptitiously obtains control over resources necessary to settle trading contracts. The manipulator then unexpectedly withdraws those resources from the

---

[5]See http://www.cfainstitute.org/ethics/codes/ethics/Pages/index.aspx.

market, which causes traders to default on their contracts, some of which the manipulator may hold. The manipulator profits by providing the resources at high prices or by closing the contracts at egregiously high prices.

For example, in short squeezes, manipulators obtain control of a substantial fraction of all available lendable stock shares or bonds. If the securities are overvalued, as they might be if the manipulators are also engaging in a pump and dump, many speculators may be short selling the securities by unknowingly borrowing them from the manipulators. The manipulators will then recall the security loans. If the short sellers ("shorts") cannot borrow the securities from others, they will be forced to buy securities in the market to cover their stock loans. Their purchases will raise prices and allow the manipulators to sell their securities at overvalued prices. Manipulators may also profit by raising the rates they charge to lend their securities. To avoid being caught in a short squeeze, short sellers must be sure that the market for lendable securities has many participants and is not concentrated in the hands of one or more entities acting in concert.

In commodity market corners, manipulators buy many futures contracts while simultaneously buying in the spot markets much of the deliverable supply of the commodity. When the contract approaches expiration, the manipulators then demand delivery from the shorts, most of whom will not own the deliverable commodity. The shorts must then buy the deliverable supply from the manipulators at egregiously high prices. Alternatively, they may repurchase their contracts from the manipulators, again at very high prices.

Corners can occur in commodity markets because most participants in commodity futures contracts do not demand to receive or make delivery when the contract expires. Instead, they close their positions by arranging offsetting trades in the futures market, either because they are simultaneously accepting or making delivery elsewhere or because they are rolling their positions into future contract months. Accordingly, most short sellers neither expect nor intend to make delivery. When forced to make delivery, they are caught short.

Corners are illegal in most jurisdictions, and they always violate the rules of the exchanges on which futures contracts trade. In general, long holders cannot demand delivery if they do not have a valid business reason for doing so. However, enforcement is complicated by the fact that manipulators may offer plausible reasons for requesting unexpected deliveries. Note also that sometimes, unexpected supply shortages coupled with unexpected legitimate demands for delivery can result in inadvertent short squeezes. Thus, short sellers who do not intend to make delivery should try to close their positions early to ensure that they are not caught in an intentional corner or an inadvertent squeeze.

## 2.4.    Liquidity Suppliers: Dealers and Arbitrageurs

*Liquidity* is the ability to trade when you want to trade *and* without much expense. Traders who supply liquidity allow other traders to trade when they want to trade. Like all other profit-motivated traders, liquidity suppliers profit by buying at lower prices than the prices at which they sell. Liquidity suppliers include dealers and arbitrageurs.

**Dealers.** *Dealers* are traders who allow their clients to buy and sell when they want to trade. They thus provide liquidity to their clients. Unlike brokers, dealers trade for their own accounts when filling their customers' orders. When dealers buy or sell, they increase or reduce their *inventories*.

Dealers profit by selling at prices higher than the prices at which they buy. The prices at which they sell are called their ask (or offer) prices, and the prices at which they buy are called their bid prices. The difference between these two prices is the bid–ask spread, which compensates dealers for their costs of doing business.

Dealing would be quite easy if prices never changed—a dealer's average profit per unit of trade would simply be half the difference between the bid and offer prices, or half the bid–ask spread. For example, suppose that a dealer buys 100 stock shares at a bid price of 20 and then sells the shares at an ask price of 22. The total profit for the round-trip transaction involving 200 shares is 200, so the average profit per unit of trade is 1, or half the bid–ask spread.

In practice, prices often change as fundamental values change—or when buyers want to buy more than sellers want to sell, or vice versa.

Imbalances of buying interest relative to selling interest are of particular concern to dealers. When faced with too much buying interest, dealers will sell out their inventories and many will even go short. To continue doing business, they must buy to restore their inventories. Likewise, when faced with too much selling interest, dealers may buy more than they want to hold or can afford to hold. To stay in business, they must sell to restore their desired inventory levels.

Dealers adjust their bid and ask prices to manage their inventories. If buying interest is greater than selling interest, dealers raise their ask prices to discourage buyers and raise their bid prices to encourage sellers. Likewise, if selling interest is greater than buying interest, dealers lower their ask prices to encourage buyers and lower their bid prices to discourage sellers.

Adjusting bid and ask prices will generally restore dealer inventory positions, but the restoration may take a long time because the changes occur only when their customers want to trade. When dealers are concerned about their inventory imbalances and are unwilling to wait for customers to arrive, they will actively trade to restore their inventories. They may arrange purchases or sales with other traders at the best available ask or bid prices. These inventory-rebalancing trades are generally costly and thus lower dealer profits.

The problem that dealers face when prices change is that they often buy when prices are falling and sell when prices are rising. They then earn less than half the spread per trade—and they may lose if rising prices cause them to buy at higher-than-expected prices or if falling prices cause them to sell at lower-than-expected prices.

For example, suppose that a dealer bids 20 and offers at 21. If many buyers arrive, the dealer will sell at 21 with the hope of repurchasing inventory at 20. But if buying interest continues to be greater than selling interest, the dealer may have to raise the offer to discourage buyers and raise the bid to encourage sellers. The dealer may even actively trade to restore the inventory. In that case, the dealer may have to repurchase inventory at 21 or higher, and the dealer will break even (if buying at 21) or lose (if buying above 21).

■ *Adverse selection.* Trading with well-informed traders is the main problem that dealers face. Well-informed traders can predict to some extent whether prices will rise or fall. They buy when they think prices will rise and sell when they think prices will fall. When trading with well-informed traders, dealers thus tend to be on the wrong side of the market, buying before prices fall and selling before prices rise. If the well-informed traders are correct, as they often are, the dealers will lose.

When possible, dealers try to avoid trading with well-informed traders, but they often do not know with whom they trade. For example, dealers who trade on exchanges generally cannot choose their counterparties. Even when dealers know their customers, they usually do not know when they are well informed. Even if they suspect that their customers are well informed, they may still trade with them to preserve their reputations as willing traders, without which they would not receive orders.

Dealers will quit if they cannot trade profitably. When faced with losses due to well-informed traders, dealers must widen their spreads to recover from all traders what they lose on average to well-informed traders. Economists call this widening of the bid–ask spread due to informed trading the *adverse selection spread* because well-informed traders select to trade on the side of the market that has adverse consequences for dealers.

The size of the adverse selection spread depends on how often dealers trade with well-informed traders and on how much they lose on average when they do. Adverse selection spreads are wide if well-informed traders represent a significant fraction of the quantities that dealers trade or if dealers generally lose a lot when trading with well-informed traders.

Dealers do not always lose when trading with well-informed traders. Although well-informed traders can predict price changes with greater accuracy than they could by simply flipping a coin, they are not always right. Also, even when well-informed traders can correctly predict future price changes, those changes may occur after dealers have restored their inventories to desired levels. If so, dealers will avoid losses.

Dealers most fear trading with news traders, who are well informed about news that will soon be public and that will cause prices to change significantly when the news becomes well known. Examples of such news include unexpected announcements of mergers and acquisitions, drug approvals and disapprovals, expropriations of assets by governments, and earnings that differ substantially from expectations. Although infrequent, these events often have large impacts on prices.

Dealers also fear trading with traders who know more about the markets than they do. For example, dealers often lose to arbitrageurs who know before they do that the prices of correlated securities have changed. When the price of the Brent crude oil contract that trades on the International Commodity Exchange (ICE) rises, the price of the light sweet crude oil (West Texas intermediate) contract that trades on the Chicago Mercantile Exchange (CME) generally also rises. Arbitrageurs who are aware of a decrease in Brent prices will buy the ICE product and sell the CME contract. These arbitrage opportunities may last for only a few milliseconds before arbitrageurs using electronic trading systems trade on them. Regardless, dealers at the CME who buy from the arbitrageurs will lose if the CME price falls as the arbitrageurs expect. The losses that dealers experience from these events tend to be very small, but they happen frequently.

The adjustment of bid and ask prices by dealers to manage their inventories explains how prices become informative in dealer markets when informed traders are trading. Dealers will be raising their prices when well-informed traders are buying, and they will be lowering their prices when well-informed traders are selling.

Note that since dealers generally cannot determine when they are trading with well-informed versus uninformed traders, they often adjust prices in response to order flow imbalances caused by uninformed traders. Such imbalances tend to move prices away from fundamental values. Eventually, value traders will recognize the discrepancy and trade on it.

**Arbitrageurs.** *Arbitrageurs* are profit-motivated traders who buy from sellers in one market while simultaneously selling to buyers interested in the same or very similar instruments in another market. Arbitrageurs thus connect buyers with sellers who are interested in trading at the same time but who are in different markets. Arbitrageurs arrange these trades when they expect that the trades will be profitable.

The markets may differ by location or by the instruments that trade there. The simplest arbitrages involve identical instruments that trade in physically separate markets. Arbitrageurs will trade when they can buy the instrument at a cheaper price in one market than they can sell it in another market. The difference between the two prices is called the arbitrage spread, the arbitrage basis, or simply the basis.

Traders also arrange arbitrages involving different instruments that represent similar risks. For example, arbitrageurs often buy (or sell) an exchange-traded fund known as the SPDR S&P 500 ETF Trust (Standard & Poor's Depositary Receipts, or "Spiders"; also known by the ticker symbol SPY) while simultaneously selling (or buying) the E-mini S&P 500 futures contract that trades at the Chicago Mercantile Exchange. Both instruments embody very similar risks—the risks of holding a stock portfolio designed to replicate the returns to the S&P 500 Index. Arbitrageurs will buy the instrument in which the price of the risk is cheaper than the price implied by the other instrument, which they will sell. In effect, the arbitrageurs convert risk from one form to the other when trading.[6]

Other arbitrageurs trade less closely related securities. For example, arbitrageurs who engage in *pairs trading* consider the normal relation between correlated securities, such as the common stocks of Ford and General Motors (GM). Both stocks embody similar risks—macroeconomic risks, industry risks, interest rate risks, and labor wage and steel price risks, among many others. Accordingly, the two stocks often move together. If one stock rises in price relative to the other, pairs traders will buy the riser and sell the other security. This strategy works when the price changes are due to trading by uninformed traders or by well-informed traders who trade only one of the

---

[6]The two instruments do not embody exactly the same risk. The SPDR is a trust that holds the S&P 500 Index portfolio. In contrast, the E-mini S&P futures contract is a contract that specifies cash flows to be exchanged among holders and writers of the contract that depend on the computed value of the S&P 500 Index. The main implication of the difference between these two instruments is that holders of the SPDR will eventually receive stock dividends paid by the S&P 500 stocks that the trust holds, whereas holders of the futures contract do not receive these dividends (and the contract value is not adjusted to account for these dividends). Thus, changes in expectations about the values of stock dividends not yet paid will have different effects on the values of these two instruments.

securities when trading on information of importance to both securities. The strategy fails when well-informed traders are trading on information specific to only one of the securities. For example, if well-informed traders believe that Ford will have to recall a product, they may sell Ford, causing its value to drop. If their information does not also suggest that GM will be required to make a similar recall, GM's price should not change.[7] Pairs traders who buy Ford and sell GM may lose if subsequent price changes confirm the expectations of the well-informed traders.

As this pairs trading example illustrates, arbitrageurs face adverse selection when they trade. They may face two types of adverse selection, depending on whether the well-informed traders are informed about company-specific factors or common factors.

The first type of adverse selection is the same type that dealers face. Like dealers, arbitrageurs may provide liquidity to well-informed traders in individual securities who are well informed with respect to company-specific factors.

The second type of adverse selection that arbitrageurs face is caused by traders who are well informed about common factor risks. Consider the trading problem that arbitrageurs face when well-informed traders believe that the values of both securities should be higher owing to an improvement in some common factor. When arbitrageurs try to sell the security that has risen, their trades will be easy to arrange because well-informed traders will be buying the security. But when arbitrageurs try to simultaneously buy the other security, their trades will be difficult and expensive to arrange because the arbitrageurs will be competing with well-informed traders to buy the security. As a result, the arbitrageurs may fail to earn the expected arbitrage spread and may even lose on the trade.

Many traders who engage in arbitrage strategies also engage in dealing strategies. Both trading strategies connect buyers with sellers. Dealing strategies connect buyers and sellers in the same market who arrive at different times. In contrast, arbitrage strategies connect buyers and sellers who arrive at the same time in different markets. Those traders who can undertake both strategies generally have an advantage over those who cannot because they have more options to successfully manage the risks associated with their trading.

---

[7]GM's price might rise if speculators think GM sales will be higher because some Ford customers concerned about quality will switch to GM products.

## 2.5. Conclusion

Besides naming and identifying the various reasons why people trade, this chapter also introduced adverse selection, one of the most important concepts in trading, and identified when the different types of informed traders profit.

Whether traders win or lose depends on how well informed they are about the future. The next chapter explains how they win or lose.

# 3. Implications of the Zero-Sum Game

Trading is a zero-sum game when gains and losses are measured relative to the market index. This chapter examines implications of this observation for investment sponsors and their investment managers.

The taxonomy of why people trade that was introduced in the last chapter, coupled with an appreciation of the implications of the zero-sum game, helps us understand when markets will exist and when active trading strategies will be successful. In particular, the distinction between profit-motivated traders and utilitarian traders has two extremely important implications:

1. Profit-motivated traders will not trade if they do not expect to profit. They simply withdraw from the market when they do not expect to profit. This observation has strong implications for dealing and arbitrage spreads and for how much information gets into prices. The profits of profit-motivated traders must be sufficiently large to cover their expenses—otherwise, they will quit. Thus, dealing and arbitrage spreads must be wide enough to allow dealers and arbitrageurs to cover their costs. Likewise, prices cannot be so informative that speculators cannot obtain a return on costly efforts to collect and process information, at least on average. When innovations cause spreads to narrow or prices to become more informative, profit-motivated trading becomes less profitable and profit-motivated traders quit.

2. Because profit-motivated traders cannot all profit if they trade only with each other, they must trade with utilitarian traders to profit. This point appeared in the Introduction (Chapter 1) and is worth repeating here, this time expressed in terms of profit-motivated traders and utilitarian traders: *Profit-motivated traders can profit only when utilitarian traders are willing to trade and, in particular, are willing to lose to them.* In one way or another, utilitarian traders lose when they incur transaction costs. They are willing to lose because they obtain benefits from trading other than trading profits. These benefits may include moving money through time (investing and borrowing), risk management (hedging), or simply entertainment.

The remainder of this chapter explains why and how uninformed traders lose to informed traders. To simplify our discussion, we will call investment managers whose financial analyses are on average informative "well-informed traders" and those whose financial analyses on average just produce random signals "uninformed traders." Well-informed traders are traders who can predict future price changes better than others can.

## 3.1. How Uninformed Traders Lose to Informed Traders

Better-informed traders profit at the expense of less-informed traders because trading is a zero-sum game. This result simply follows from an accounting identity. By itself, this result is not particularly useful to uninformed traders seeking to minimize their losses to informed traders. To understand how to do so, uninformed traders must know exactly how they lose to well-informed traders. Understanding this mechanism requires that we consider the origins of transaction costs. For that, we must discuss adverse selection further.

**Adverse Selection Harms Uninformed Traders.** Assume that well-informed traders want to buy a security. Remembering that uninformed traders buy or sell with roughly equal probability, contrast what happens when uninformed traders are sellers with what happens when they are buyers.

When uninformed traders are sellers, they will trade with the well-informed traders. Their trades will be easy to arrange, and the costs of trading will be low for both types of traders. The uninformed traders will be on the wrong side of the market on average and will lose. The well-informed traders will be on the right side on average and will profit.

Now suppose that the uninformed traders are buyers. Both types of traders are on the same side of the market, and they will be competing against each other to find sellers willing to sell to them. Their competition will typically push prices higher as they try to attract sellers. All buyers—well informed or otherwise—who ultimately trade will be on the right side of the market and all will profit on average (assuming that they have not pushed prices above value). Those buyers who are unable to trade will lose the opportunity to profit.

To summarize, the well-informed traders will win on average regardless of whether the uninformed traders are buyers or sellers. Well-informed traders win because they can predict with some accuracy in which direction prices will move.

The uninformed traders lose when by chance they are on the wrong side of the market, and they win otherwise. But note that the uninformed traders' transaction costs are higher on the winning side than on the losing side. Without transaction costs, uninformed traders would break even on average. With transaction costs, uninformed traders lose on average.

The asymmetry in transaction costs that uninformed traders face when informed traders are present causes uninformed traders to lose on average. Economists call these losses *adverse selection losses* because they are due to the well-informed traders' ability to select which side of the market to be on and because their selection is adverse to the welfare of other traders.

**Adverse Selection Also Harms Dealers.** Uninformed traders incur adverse selection losses even when they trade through dealers and not directly with well-informed traders. Uninformed traders lose because the dealers lose to the informed traders and the dealers pass those losses on to the uninformed traders through higher spreads.

Dealers are in the business of offering liquidity to other traders. They allow other traders to trade when they want to trade. They expect to profit by buying at their bid prices and selling at their higher offer prices, which are also known as their ask prices. The difference between their bid and offer prices is called their bid–ask spread.

Dealers lose when prices drop after they buy or rise after they sell. To reduce the risk of such losses, dealers try to sell quickly after they buy and buy quickly after they sell. In particular, they try to arrange their trading so that their inventories—the quantities that they hold in the various securities in which they trade—do not become too large or too small.

Dealers are especially vulnerable to informed traders because dealers are on the wrong side of the market when well-informed traders trade with them: On average, prices rise when well-informed traders buy and fall when they sell. Dealers lose if they cannot offset their trades before prices change as the well-informed traders expect. For example, if well-informed traders expect that prices will fall, they will sell to dealers. The dealers will lose if they cannot sell those positions to other traders before prices fall. Dealers thus lose on average to well-informed traders.

To stay in business, dealers must widen their bid–ask spreads so that they recover from all traders what they lose on average to well-informed traders. Academics call this additional widening of the bid–ask spread the *adverse selection spread component*. It compensates the dealers for their losses when well-informed traders select the side of the market on which to trade that is adverse to the dealers' interests.

The adverse selection spread explains why uninformed traders lose to well-informed traders when they trade through dealers. They lose because they have to pay wider spreads to trade than they otherwise would pay if dealers did not lose on average to well-informed traders. Note again that uninformed traders will win when by chance they buy securities that outperform the market or sell securities that underperform the market. They likewise will lose when by chance they buy securities that underperform the market or sell securities that outperform the market. On average, these gains and losses will cancel out. But on all these trades, uninformed traders pay transaction costs to dealers when they buy at ask prices and sell at lower bid prices. These transaction costs cause their losses to be roughly proportional to their total trading volumes. Uninformed traders can minimize these losses by simply trading less often. These losses are largest when well-informed traders expose dealers to much adverse selection, which results in wide dealer spreads.

## 3.2. Conclusion

The discussion in this chapter shows that uninformed traders lose on average to well-informed traders simply because they trade. If they trade directly with informed traders, they are on the wrong side of the market. If they trade on the same side, their orders tend not to execute or their executions are costly. And if they trade via the intermediation of dealers, they lose through their transaction costs because dealers must charge spreads that allow them to recoup from all traders what they lose to informed traders.

For uninformed traders, the single most important determinant of their overall transaction costs is the decision to trade. Uninformed traders who do not trade do not lose to informed traders. This observation explains why passive buy-and-hold investment strategies, such as indexing, have grown so popular in recent years.

# 4. Transaction Cost Measurement and Management

Effective control of transaction costs requires that they be measured. As with all other processes, you cannot manage what you cannot measure.

Buy-side traders measure transaction costs for multiple purposes:

- To determine whether their brokers are working effectively on their behalf and to confirm that they are getting value for their brokerage commissions

- To determine whether they should be trading more or less aggressively

- To better understand whether they are competing with other traders who are trading on the same information

- To inform their portfolio managers about liquidity conditions in various securities

Developers of electronic trading systems also measure transaction costs. The design and fine-tuning of trading algorithms and order-routing systems that buy-side traders, proprietary traders, and brokers use require that their developers accurately predict trade execution costs for various trading strategies and venues. To that end, developers study the executions of past orders. They also occasionally design and conduct live trading experiments to generate reliable information about issues of particular concern to them.

The costs of trading include fixed costs and variable costs. For buy-side institutions, *fixed trading costs* include the costs of employing buy-side traders, the costs of equipping them with proper trading tools (electronic systems and data), and the costs of office space (trading rooms or corners). Small buy-side institutions often avoid these costs by not employing buy-side traders. Their portfolio managers submit their orders directly to their brokers.

*Variable transaction costs* consist of explicit and implicit transaction costs. *Explicit transaction costs* are easy to measure—they primarily include commissions, exchange fees, and transaction taxes.

*Implicit transaction costs* are due to the market impact of trading. Buyers often must raise prices to encourage sellers to trade with them, and sellers often must lower prices to encourage buyers. The price concessions that impatient traders make to complete their trades are called the *market impacts* of their trades. For small orders, market impact is often limited to buying at bid prices and selling at lower ask prices. Larger orders have greater market impact when traders must move the market to fill their orders.

Implicit transaction costs are often negative for patient traders who offer liquidity (i.e., post standing limit orders that allow others to trade when they want to trade). The decision to take or offer liquidity thus is a very important determinant of overall transaction costs. The decision is not easy, however: Traders who offer liquidity take the risk that they may fail to trade when they wish they had. For example, if the market is 20 bid, offered at 21, a trader who offers to sell at 21 using a limit 21 sell order may fail to trade if the market drops. If the trader still wants to sell, the trader will have to sell at a lower price, possibly lower than the 20 bid price at which the trader might have sold had the trader initially demanded liquidity with a market order.

Implicit transaction costs are often hard to measure, especially for large orders. The body of this chapter addresses the problem of measuring implicit transaction costs. The chapter concludes by identifying how portfolio managers and their buy-side traders can improve overall performance by exchanging information about liquidity needs and liquidity conditions.

## 4.1. Measuring Implicit Transaction Costs

To measure implicit transaction costs, transaction cost analysts must determine how good trade prices are. For buy orders, good trade prices are low prices; for sell orders, good trade prices are high prices. Analysts estimate transaction costs by comparing trade prices with *benchmark prices* that provide some characterization of market conditions. In particular, they estimate transaction costs using the following simple formula:

$$Transaction\ cost\ estimate = Trade\ size \times \begin{cases} Trade\ price - Benchmark\ price\ \text{for buy orders} \\ Benchmark\ price - Trade\ price\ \text{for sell orders} \end{cases},$$

where the trade price is the volume-weighted average trade price if the order is executed in two or more trades.

The transaction costs that analysts estimate thus depend on the benchmark prices they use. The next three subsections describe the three most commonly used benchmarks and the properties of the resulting transaction cost estimators.

**Effective Spreads (Midquote Price Benchmark).** For small orders, analysts often use the midquote price (the average of the bid and the ask prices) as the benchmark price:

$$\textit{Effective spread transaction cost estimate} = \textit{Trade size} \times \begin{cases} \textit{Trade price} - \dfrac{\textit{Bid} + \textit{Ask}}{2} \text{ for buy orders} \\[2ex] \dfrac{\textit{Bid} + \textit{Ask}}{2} - \textit{Trade price} \text{ for sell orders} \end{cases}.$$

Thus, the estimated implicit cost of trading a buy order at the ask is half the bid–ask spread because $Ask - (Bid + Ask / 2) = (Ask - Bid / 2)$.

Multiplying this midquote price benchmark transaction cost estimate by 2 produces a statistic called the *effective spread*. It is the spread that would have been observed if the quoted ask (for a purchase) or the bid (for a sale) were equal to the trade price.

The effective spread is a sensible estimate of transaction costs when orders are filled in single trades. If an order fills at a price better than the quoted price (e.g., a buy order that fills at a price below the asking price), the order is said to receive price improvement and the spread is effectively lower. An order that fills at a price outside the quoted spread has an effective spread that is larger than the quoted spread.

The effective spread is a poor estimate of transaction costs when traders split large orders into many parts to fill over time. Such orders often move the market and cause bid and ask prices to rise or fall. The impact of the order on market prices makes trading expensive—especially for the last parts to fill, but the effective spread will not fully identify this cost if it is computed separately for each trade.

For example, suppose that a buy order for 10,000 shares fills in two trades. The prices and sizes of these trades and the best bids and offers in the market when the trades occurred appear in the following table:

| Trade | Trade Price | Trade Size | Prevailing Bid | Prevailing Offer |
|-------|-------------|------------|----------------|------------------|
| #1 | 10.21 | 4,000 | 10.19 | 10.21 |
| #2 | 10.22 | 6,000 | 10.20 | 10.22 |

For this buy order, the transaction cost per share is 0.01 for both trades (the effective spreads are both 0.02), and thus the total transaction cost estimate measured using the midquote price benchmark is 100. This estimate is problematic because it does not take into account the higher price of the second trade, which may have been due to the buyer's demand for liquidity.

**Implementation Shortfall (Initial Midquote Price Benchmark).** An obvious solution to this problem is to compute the total transaction cost estimate using only the first midquote price. This method is called the *implementation shortfall* method of estimating transaction costs. (The complete implementation shortfall method also estimates opportunity costs of not trading, discussed later.) In this case, the implementation shortfall transaction cost estimate is $160 = 4,000 \times (10.21 - 10.20) + 6,000 \times (10.22 - 10.20)$, which is higher than the total effective spread cost estimate, as expected.

Analysts can also compute the implementation shortfall transaction cost estimate from the difference between the volume-weighted average execution price and the benchmark price. In our example, the volume-weighted average price is $10.216 = 4,000 \div (4,000 + 6,000) \times 10.21 + 6,000 \div (4,000 + 6,000) \times 10.22$. The implementation shortfall estimated from this average price is $160 = 10,000 \times (10.216 - 10.20)$.

One problem with the implementation shortfall transaction cost estimation method is that changes in price following the first execution of an order may be due to factors unrelated to the execution of the order. For example, if the market as a whole rises while the order is being filled, the stock may also rise. If it does, the order will appear to have been very expensive to fill. Conversely, if the market falls, the estimated transaction cost may be low or even negative.

Counting these market moves in the transaction cost estimate would be sensible only if the trader could reasonably be expected to anticipate them. If so, the trader could (and should) lower the total costs of trading by accelerating the execution of buy orders when the trader expects prices will rise and by delaying their execution when the trader expects prices will fall—and conversely for sell orders. However, few traders have these short-term forecasting skills, and those who do typically work for high-frequency traders rather than buy-side institutions.

Implementation shortfall transaction cost estimates thus will be noisy when prices move for unanticipated reasons unrelated to the order. Transaction cost analysts can remove some of this noise by using benchmark prices that they adjust for security price changes that are correlated with index price changes. Generally, such estimates will more accurately reflect transaction costs, but for any given trade, these adjustments may improperly increase or decrease transaction cost estimates if the security does not move with the market as expected. If the errors are equally likely to be positive or negative, as would be expected when markets are informationally efficient, they should cancel out over time such that average transaction cost estimates computed over many orders should reliably estimate true transaction costs.

When computing implementation shortfall transaction cost estimates, many analysts use the midquote price at the time the decision to trade was made (or if unavailable, the time the order was created) as the price benchmark instead of the midquote price associated with the first executed trade. This price is called the *decision price*. Computing implementation shortfall transaction cost estimates from decision prices allows analysts to examine how prices change between the creation of the order and the first execution. If prices generally rise over this interval for buy orders (or fall for sell orders), traders should be able to reduce their transaction costs by trading faster. This price pattern is often observed when traders are competing with other traders who are trading on the same information. Under such circumstances, the first to the market will obtain the better trade prices.

More generally, transaction cost analysts often produce studies of price changes surrounding decisions to trade. The pattern of prices before the decision to trade can indicate whether the orders are generated from momentum or contrarian strategies and may suggest modifications to the trade decision process. For example, if prices tend to rise before the decision to purchase is made, portfolio managers, whether they know it or not, are pursuing a momentum trading strategy, at least in the short term. The momentum may be caused by other traders acting more quickly than they are on the same information. In that case, the portfolio managers must speed up their decision processes to obtain better performance.

The pattern of prices after the first trade can also provide information about how best to split up an order. For example, if prices tend to rise quickly following the first trade, it may be best to trade a greater fraction of the order in earlier trades than in later trades.

**Market VWAP Benchmark.** The most common benchmark used to compute transaction costs is the volume-weighted average price (VWAP) of all trades that occur in the market, computed over some interval during which the order was filled. Often, this interval is the day on which the order was filled. Analysts sometimes also compute the VWAP over the period between the first and last trades that filled the order. VWAP transaction cost estimates are intuitively attractive because they answer the question, Compared with all other buyers (or sellers) participating in the market when I was trading, how well did I trade?

Although intuitively compelling, transaction cost estimates based on the market VWAP benchmark suffer from some very serious problems:

1. Market VWAP transaction cost estimates tend to be near zero when traders split up their orders to participate uniformly in market trading activity. *VWAP trading algorithms* implement this trading strategy. The VWAPs of trades arranged by VWAP algorithms are approximately equal to market VWAPs measured over the execution periods. This result is unattractive because the orders may have substantial price impact that the VWAP method does not measure. For example, suppose that a large trader raises prices 50%, from 10 to 15, while buying, and suppose further for illustrative clarity that the trader was the only buyer that day. The trade is clearly very expensive, but the trader's VWAP and the market VWAP will be exactly equal and thus the estimated transaction cost is zero. The problem is quite serious since many large traders use VWAP algorithms specifically because they want to obtain VWAP prices over the execution period and thus appear to trade at low cost. The desire of traders and investment managers to look good in front of their clients probably explains why the VWAP transaction cost method is so popular.

2. Market VWAP transaction cost estimates tend to be positive for traders filling orders generated by momentum strategies. Momentum strategies generate buy orders when markets are rising and sell orders when markets are falling. If the period during which the market VWAP is computed includes trades that occurred before the decision to trade was made, the market VWAP will be below the decision price for buy orders and above for sell orders. Subsequent executions thus appear very costly in comparison with the market VWAP. Such transaction cost estimates reveal more about the decisions to trade than about the costs of implementing those decisions. (A similar analysis shows that the VWAP method underestimates transaction costs for orders generated by contrarian strategies if the market VWAP includes pre-decision trades.)

3. Market VWAP transaction cost estimates tend to be negative for orders that reflect information that will soon have an impact on market prices. If the period during which the market VWAP is computed includes trades that occurred after the order was filled and if prices subsequently move in the expected direction, the trade will appear to be very cheap. Such transaction cost estimates reveal more about the decisions to trade than about the costs of implementing those decisions.

4. Finally, if analysts estimate transaction costs separately for each day that an order executes, brokers may be tempted to manipulate the VWAP measure. For example, suppose that a broker receives a large order to buy stock just before the end of the day. Suppose further that the stock price that day dropped substantially such that the VWAP for the day is now significantly above current market prices. The broker may be tempted to fill the entire buy order quickly without regard to the true costs of filling the order because even poor trade prices will look good compared with the higher earlier prices. Without this temptation, the broker might fill only a portion of the order and try to fill more the next day. In contrast, suppose that the stock price that day rose substantially such that the VWAP for the day is significantly below current market prices. Now the broker might be tempted not to fill the buy order, even if the broker could easily fill it with little impact on price, since even a great price at the end of the day will look like a poor price compared with earlier prices.

The problems discussed in points 2, 3, and 4 suggest that VWAP transaction cost analyses are best undertaken using a market VWAP benchmark that is computed from all market prices observed between the times of order creation and last fill. In practice, order creation times (decision times) often are not recorded, and thus many analyses can use only the time of the first fill. Note, however, that when the only trades in the market during the analysis interval are those arranged to fill the order—as is always the case when the entire order is filled in one trade—the VWAP estimate will be zero.

Like implementation shortfall transaction cost estimates, VWAP transaction cost estimates are influenced by price changes that are unrelated to the execution of the order. The impact of unexpected price changes will be lower for the VWAP method because traders often spread their fills out over time. Of course, as noted in point 1, this behavior also ensures that the VWAP method will not measure market impact.

**Opportunity Costs.** Traders often stop filling orders when prices have moved so far away from their decision prices that they are no longer interested in trading. If any parts of the unfilled portions of their orders—called the *remainders*—could have been traded but were not, the traders suffer lost trade opportunities. Transaction cost analysts study the costs of lost trading opportunities to help traders understand whether they are trading too aggressively or not aggressively enough.

For example, suppose that a trader decides to buy 100,000 shares of a security using a limit 30 order when the midquote price is 28. As a result of buying pressure exerted by the trader and possibly by other traders also buying the same security, the price rises to 35 over several days. If the trader trades only 60,000 shares before the price passes through 30, the trader will wish that he had traded the remaining 40,000 shares. If the trader could have traded the remaining shares, the trader will have lost the opportunity to earn at least 200,000 = 40,000 × (35 – 30), and possibly more.

Likewise, when sellers fail to trade the full sizes of their orders when prices are falling, they lose the opportunity to avoid losses (if they are selling from long positions) or to profit (if they are selling short).

Analysts try to assign values to these lost opportunities. The resulting estimates are called *opportunity cost estimates.*

To estimate opportunity costs, analysts must choose a benchmark price and a *valuation price* at which the remainder will be valued (in the previous example, the valuation price is 35), and they must specify how much size the trader reasonably could have been expected to fill.

- *The benchmark price.* Analysts using the implementation shortfall method to estimate opportunity costs generally use the decision price as the benchmark price.

- *The final valuation price.* Analysts usually assume that the valuation price is the price observed at the end of some prespecified period following the final trade of the order—for example, at the end of the day a week after the last trade. Noise in opportunity cost estimates increases with the time to the observation of the valuation price.

- *The unfilled remainder.* To estimate opportunity costs, analysts must also estimate what fraction of the order truly could have been traded. Opportunity costs clearly are meaningless if the order was so large that no strategy would have allowed the trader to completely fill the order. In our example, if the analyst believed that it was only reasonable to expect that a total of 70,000 shares could be purchased, the opportunity costs should be computed only on the 10,000-share difference between the expected 70,000-share purchase and the actual 60,000-share purchase. The remaining 30,000 shares presumably represent an unrealistic hope of the portfolio manager.

Although estimating opportunity costs is clearly quite challenging, the results can be extremely valuable for fine-tuning trading processes. When realistically estimated opportunity costs are large relative to transaction costs, traders can produce more value by trading more aggressively. More aggressive trading strategies will decrease opportunity costs and increase transaction costs. The optimal strategy is to be aggressive up to the point where the increase in transaction costs from being a bit more aggressive is just equal to the decrease in opportunity costs.

In practice, most traders are unable to do this calculation because they lack the required information. But those traders who are aware of the need to balance transaction costs with opportunity costs will undoubtedly make better decisions in the long run than those who do not even think about the problem.

**Final Comments.** Transaction cost analysts—especially those who work for companies that provide transaction cost consulting services, such as ITG and Ancerno—often use regression models to obtain the predicted costs of filling orders. These models characterize how transaction cost estimates for a set of completed trades depend on variables such as order size, average daily volume, volatility, and recent past price changes, among many others. The predicted values from these regressions provide useful benchmarks for evaluating transaction cost estimates. In particular, they help analysts determine whether a trader was able to obtain better executions on average after considering the difficulty of the trading problem. Of course, any biases in the transaction cost estimates will also affect these regression analyses.

Transaction cost analysts must fully understand the transaction data that they analyze. Most importantly, they must know when trades are part of the same order. Without such information, analysts will underestimate the market impacts of large orders. Analysts must also recognize that managers sometimes add to the sizes of their buy orders if prices fall during the course of their executions and add to the sizes of their sell orders if prices rise. This behavior is normal for many value-motivated investors, but it can lead to underestimation of transaction costs for both implementation shortfall and VWAP if the managers do not create and record new orders when adding size. If managers add to the size of their original orders before the data are analyzed, the resulting transaction cost estimates will underestimate the true transaction costs because the additional size will execute at favorable prices compared with the benchmark price.

In practice, transaction cost estimates for individual orders are often quite noisy regardless of the benchmark method used. They become useful when averaged over many orders, because averaging tends to reduce the influence of noise on the results.

Finally, note that the sum of implementation shortfall transaction costs and implementation shortfall opportunity costs is equal to the difference between (1) the profits that a trader would have earned if the entire order could have been executed at the decision price (called *paper profits* because they are not real) and (2) the actual profits earned from executing the orders. The implementation shortfall transaction cost estimation method is sometimes called the *method of paper portfolios* because of its relation to paper profits. It is called implementation shortfall because the profits associated with implementing trading decisions generally fall short of the paper profits. The difference is due to the costs of both trading and failing to trade.

## 4.2. Communications among Buy-Side Traders and Portfolio Managers

To create optimal trading strategies, buy-side traders need to know why their portfolio managers want to trade. If their portfolio managers are trading on information with the expectation that others will soon know what they know, the buy-side traders must trade aggressively to fill their orders before the market moves away and the profit opportunity disappears. In this circumstance, high transaction costs, while always undesirable, are often acceptable. Otherwise, traders may incur large opportunity costs. This example illustrates that the object of trading is not to minimize transaction costs but, rather, to minimize the total implementation shortfall.

In contrast, when managers know that their orders are not motivated by information that will soon be public and, further, that other traders are not likely to be trading on the same information, their traders might choose to trade patiently and wait for the market to come to them. This situation might arise if the desired trade were a sale motivated by the need to produce liquidity to fund some other transaction.

Portfolio managers also need to know information that traders can best provide. In particular, traders can tell managers how expensive trading certain securities will be. Managers need this information to decide how to allocate limited research budgets, because investing heavily in research about the values of securities that cannot be easily traded is often foolish. Managers also need to know about liquidity conditions so they can choose reasonable sizes for their orders. Finally, buy-side traders often become aware of trading opportunities that might interest their portfolio managers if the managers knew about them. For example, managers sometimes are interested in buying large blocks of securities if they can do so with low transaction costs, whereas they might not be interested in acquiring similar positions a little at a time.

# 5. Electronic Trading

Trading at organized exchanges now depends critically on automated electronic systems used both by exchanges and by their trader clients. The exchanges use electronic systems to arrange trades by matching orders submitted by buyers with those submitted by sellers. Many traders—especially dealers and arbitrageurs—use electronic systems to generate the orders that the exchanges process.

The two types of systems are co-dependent: Traders need high-speed order processing and communication systems to implement their electronic trading strategies, and the exchanges need electronic exchange systems to process the huge numbers of orders that these electronic traders produce. The adoption of electronic exchange systems led to huge growth in automated order creation and submission systems.

The widespread use of electronic trading systems significantly decreased trading costs for buy-side traders. Costs fell as exchanges obtained greater cost efficiencies from using electronic matching systems instead of floor-based manual trading systems. These technologies also decreased costs and increased efficiencies for the dealers and arbitrageurs who provide much of the liquidity offered at exchanges. Competition forced them to pass along much of the benefits of their new technologies to buy-side traders in the form of narrower spreads quoted for larger sizes. New electronic buy-side order management systems also decreased buy-side trading costs by allowing a smaller number of buy-side traders to process more orders and to process them more efficiently than manual traders.

This chapter discusses how innovative electronic trading systems—and the trading strategies that they facilitate—decreased buy-side transaction costs. The discussion also considers some strategies that high-speed traders use to exploit other traders and the means by which traders can protect themselves from losses to these parasitic traders.

The discussion starts with a brief identification of the reasons why exchanges adopted electronic trade matching systems and lists the various types of electronic traders in the markets and the strategies that they use when trading. Next, the reasons why speed is important to the strategies' successful implementation are enumerated and the methods that high-speed traders use to speed their trading are described. Finally, I explain why computerized trading has been so successful.

## 5.1. Fast Electronic Exchange Trading Systems

Compared with floor-based trading systems, electronic order-matching systems enjoy many advantages:

- Most obviously, electronic systems are very cheap to operate once built. Operating in server rooms, they require less physical space than do trading floors. That space need not need be lit, designed to safely and comfortably accommodate hundreds or thousands of workers, or regularly cleaned to remove discarded order tickets and pizza boxes. Also, in contrast to floor-based trading systems, electronic trading systems do not require exchange officials to record and report prices.

- Electronic exchange systems do exactly what they are programmed to do. When properly programmed, they precisely enforce the exchange's trading order precedence and pricing rules without error or exception, and they never favor friends or confederates.

- Electronic exchange systems can also keep perfect audit trails so that forensic investigators can determine the exact sequence and timing of events that may interest them.

- Electronic exchange systems that support hidden orders keep those orders perfectly hidden. Unlike floor brokers, they have "perfect poker faces," so they never inadvertently or fraudulently reveal their clients' hidden orders to friends or confederates.

- In contrast to floor-based brokers and exchange officials, electronic order-matching systems do not get tired, call in sick, complain about their bonuses, or drop pizza crumbs into their keyboards.

- Finally, electronic exchanges can operate when bad weather or other events would likely prevent workers from convening on a floor.

These efficiencies led to great growth. Electronic trading systems have largely displaced floor-based trading systems in all instruments for which order-driven markets are viable.[8]

---

[8]Order-driven markets are markets that arrange trades using order precedence rules to match buy orders with sell orders and trade-pricing rules to assign prices to the trades thus arranged. Almost all exchange markets are order-driven markets.

## 5.2. Types of Electronic Traders

The proliferation of exchange electronic trading systems has led to the adoption of electronic trading strategies by proprietary traders, buy-side traders, and the electronic brokers that serve them. Proprietary traders include dealers, arbitrageurs, and various types of front runners—all of whom are profit-motivated traders. In contrast, buy-side traders trade to fill orders for investment and risk managers who use the markets to establish positions from which they derive various utilitarian and profit-motivated benefits. Electronic brokers serve both types of traders.

Electronic traders differ in how they send orders to markets. Those proprietary traders who are registered as broker-dealers generally send their orders directly to exchanges. Those who are not broker-dealers usually must send their orders to brokers who then forward them to exchanges. These brokers are said to provide *sponsored access* to their electronic proprietary trader clients. Brokers who provide sponsored access have very fast electronic order processing systems that allow them to forward orders to exchanges as quickly as possible while still undertaking the regulatory functions necessary to protect the markets and themselves from various financial and operational risks associated with brokering orders for electronic proprietary traders.

Electronic trading strategies are most profitable or effective when they can act on new information quickly. Accordingly, proprietary traders and electronic brokers build automated trading systems that are extremely fast. These systems often can receive information of interest to the trader, process it, and place a trading instruction at an exchange in less than a few milliseconds (one-thousandth of a second), and sometimes much faster. The elapsed time between an event and an action that depends on that event is the *latency* of a system (Section 5.4 describes how engineers build low-latency trading systems).

The events that interest electronic traders include

- trade reports and quote changes in the securities or contracts that they trade,

- similar data for instruments that are correlated with the securities or contracts that they trade,

- indexes that summarize these data across markets and for various instrument classes,

- changes in limit order books, and

- news releases from companies, governments, and other producers and aggregators of information.

Electronic traders typically receive information about these events via high-speed electronic data feeds. Not all electronic traders analyze all these different information sources, but many do.

**Electronic Proprietary Traders.** Electronic proprietary traders include high-frequency traders and low-latency traders. Both must often trade very quickly in response to new information to be profitable. They are distinguished by how often they trade.

*High-frequency traders* (HFTs) generally complete round trips composed of a purchase followed by a sale (or a sale followed by a purchase) within a minute and often as quickly as a few milliseconds. During the course of a day, they may trade in and out of an actively traded security or contract more than a thousand times, but usually only in small sizes. The most common high-frequency-trading strategies are dealing and arbitrage.

*Low-latency traders* include news traders who trade on electronic news feeds and certain parasitic traders such as front runners and quote matchers. When trying to open or close positions, they often need to send or cancel orders very quickly in response to new information. In contrast to HFTs, low-latency traders may hold their positions for as long as a day and sometimes longer.

The distinction between HFTs and low-latency traders is relatively new. Many commentators do not make any distinction, calling all electronic traders who need to trade quickly HFTs.

*Electronic news traders* subscribe to high-speed electronic news feeds that report news releases made by corporations, governments, and other aggregators of information. They then quickly analyze these releases to determine whether the information they contain will move the markets and, if so, in which direction. They trade on this information by sending marketable orders to wherever they expect they may be filled. News traders profit when they can execute against stale orders—orders that do not yet reflect the new information.

For example, stock prices usually rise when a company announces earnings of 25 pence a share when the consensus forecast is only 10 pence. Electronic news traders who receive the initial press release will use their computers to parse the text of the release to find the earnings number. The computers then will compare that number with the consensus forecast, which they have stored in their memory rather than on disk to reduce access time. Assuming that the 15 pence difference is sufficiently large, news traders may send one or more marketable buy orders to exchanges for execution.

News traders must be very quick to ensure that they get to the market before others do. If they are too late, the price may have already changed or liquidity suppliers may have canceled their quotes.

To trade profitably, news traders also must correctly parse the news releases to identify the information of interest to them. For example, news traders who trade on earnings releases study past earnings releases of the company in question as well as those of other companies to identify how companies typically present their earnings numbers. News traders must be sure that they identify the earnings numbers that interest them and not those earnings numbers presented on a different accounting basis that may also appear in the release.

Some news traders also process news releases that do not contain quantitative data. Using natural language processing techniques, they try to identify the importance of the information for market valuations. For example, a report stating that "our main pesticide plant shut down due to the accidental release of poisonous chemicals" might be marked as having strong negative implications for values. Electronic news traders would sell on this information. If they are correct, the market will drop as other, slower traders read, interpret, and act on the information. If they are wrong, the market will not react to the information. If so, news traders will reverse their position, and they will lose the transaction costs associated with their round-trip trades. (Note that these transaction costs could be high if many news traders made the same wrong inference.) Because round-trip transaction costs for most stocks are not high for small to moderately sized trades compared with the profits that electronic news traders can occasionally make when significant news arrives, news traders may trade often with the expectation of being right occasionally.

*Electronic dealers*, like all dealers, make markets by placing bids and offers with the expectation that they can profit from round trips at favorable net spreads. Those who trade at the highest frequencies tend to be very skittish. On the first indication that prices may move against their inventories (down if they are long, up if short), they immediately take liquidity on the opposite side to reduce their exposure. They will generally not hold large inventory positions—usually less than $50,000 per stock in actively traded stocks. As soon as they reach their inventory limit on one side of the market or the other, they cease bidding or offering on that side. Electronic dealers are profitable more often when they trade as market makers than as market takers and when they do not lose too much on their inventories.

Electronic dealers often monitor electronic news feeds. They may immediately cancel all their orders in any security mentioned in a news report. If the news is material, they do not want to offer liquidity to news traders. If the news is immaterial, they merely lose whatever opportunity to trade may have come their way while out of the market.

Electronic dealers, like all other dealers, also keep track of scheduled news releases. They cancel their orders just before releases to avoid offering liquidity to traders who can act faster than they can. They also may try to flatten their inventories before a scheduled release to avoid holding a risky position. For example, trading in interest rate futures markets often slows substantially just before the Bureau of Labor Statistics of the US Department of Labor releases its various monthly reports on employment and unemployment at 10:00 a.m. (ET), usually on Tuesdays or Wednesdays.

*Electronic arbitrageurs* look across markets for arbitrage opportunities in which they can buy an undervalued instrument and sell a similar overvalued one. The combination of these two positions is called an *arbitrage portfolio*, and the positions are called *legs*. Electronic arbitrageurs try to construct their arbitrage portfolios at minimum cost and risk, using three trading strategies that vary by cost and risk.

1. *Take liquidity on both sides.* The most costly and least risky arbitrage trading strategy involves using marketable orders to fill both legs. This strategy is profitable only if the arbitrage spread is sufficiently large, but competition among arbitrageurs ensures that such large arbitrage spreads are quite rare. Arbitrageurs can seldom simultaneously take liquidity in two markets for identical instruments and make a profit. To effectively execute this strategy, arbitrageurs must use very fast trading systems so that they can lock in the arbitrage spread before prices in one or both markets change.

2. *Offer liquidity on one side.* In this strategy, arbitrageurs offer liquidity in one or both of the markets in which they trade. When they obtain a fill in one market, they immediately take liquidity in the other market to complete the construction of their arbitrage portfolio. This strategy produces lower-cost executions, but it is a bit riskier than the first strategy.

For example, suppose that Markets A and B are both quoting 20 bid, offered at 21 for the same instrument. An arbitrageur may place a bid at 19 in Market A with the hope that a large seller will come along who takes all liquidity at 20 in Market A and then proceeds to fill the arbitrageur's order at 19. If so, the arbitrageur will immediately try to sell to the 20 bid in Market B. If the arbitrageur is quick enough, he may be able to fill his order before the bidder at 20 in Market B cancels that bid and before any other trader—particularly the large trader—takes it. Needless to say, the arbitrageur will immediately cancel his 19 bid in Market A if the 20 bid in Market B disappears.

Arbitrageurs often use a similar strategy when engaged in pairs trading. When they want to arrange a pair of arbitrage trades, they may offer liquidity in both stocks by placing a limit order to buy the stock they perceive as undervalued and another limit order to sell the stock they perceive as overvalued. As soon as one order executes, they will immediately cancel the other order and replace it with a market order or an immediately marketable limit order. As in the first strategy, arbitrageurs must lock in the arbitrage spread before prices in the second market change. When successfully implemented, this strategy allows arbitrageurs to obtain midpoint executions, on average, in both securities.[9] To effectively execute this second strategy, arbitrageurs must use very fast trading systems so they can cancel limit orders and replace them with marketable orders before their limit orders execute and before prices change in the market in which they intend to take liquidity.

3. *Offer liquidity on both sides.* The final arbitrage strategy involves offering liquidity in both markets. In this strategy, after the first order to execute fills, the arbitrageur continues to offer liquidity to complete the second trade. This strategy is the riskiest strategy because arbitrageurs are exposed to substantial price risk when one leg is filled and the other is

---

[9]Suppose that an arbitrageur believes that the normal relation between the price changes in two similar stocks should be 2:1—if the price of one stock goes up by 1, the price of the other should eventually go up by 2. Suppose further that the market for Stock A initially is 20 bid, offered at 21, and the market for Stock B is 45 bid, offered at 47. If Stock A ticks up to 21 bid, offered at 22, the arbitrageur expects that the market for Stock B will change to 47 bid, offered at 49, or that the market for Stock A will revert to 20 bid, offered at 21. Now suppose that neither market changes, leading the arbitrageur to believe that Stock B is undervalued relative to Stock A. Thus, the arbitrageur would like to buy Stock B and sell Stock A.

If the arbitrageur takes liquidity in both markets (buys Stock B at 47 and sells Stock A at 21), the arbitrageur will not profit. Following these arbitrage trades, if Stock B rises to 47 bid, offered at 49, to reflect the new valuation of Stock A, the arbitrageur will be able to sell his position in Stock A (bought at 47) at 47 for no profit but will lose if he tries to repurchase Stock A (sold at 21) by taking liquidity at 22, and he will break even if he can repurchase Stock A by offering liquidity at 21. Alternatively, following these arbitrage trades, if Stock A reverts to 20 bid, offered at 21 (and Stock B remains unchanged at 45 bid, offered at 47), the arbitrageur will be able to repurchase Stock A (sold at 21) with no profit but will lose if he tries to sell Stock B (bought at 47) by taking liquidity at 45, and he will break even if he can sell Stock B by offering liquidity at 21.

Instead, the arbitrageur will either wait until the arbitrage spread widens further or place limit orders to sell Stock A at 22 and to buy Stock B at 45. As soon as one order executes, the arbitrageur will cancel the other order and replace it with a marketable order, thereby obtaining a midpoint execution, on average, in both securities.

not. Moreover, if prices are moving because well-informed traders are on the same side in both markets—as they might be if the well-informed traders possess information about common risk factors—the leg providing liquidity to the informed traders will fill quickly whereas the other leg will be difficult and expensive to fill.

Arbitrageurs using this strategy trade much like dealers. Like dealers, they may switch from offering liquidity to taking liquidity when they believe that offering liquidity may be too risky. They may also often cancel and resubmit their orders when market conditions change. Thus, they are most effective when they use fast trading systems.

When the arbitrage spread reverts, as the arbitrageurs expect, the arbitrageurs will reverse their trades, often using the same strategy they used to acquire their arbitrage portfolios. Of course, if the spread never reverts, arbitrageurs will lose regardless of how they trade. They will lose less, however, if they can trade their arbitrage portfolio by offering liquidity in one or both legs.

*Electronic front runners* are low-latency traders who use artificial intelligence methods to identify when large traders, or a large number of small traders, are trying to fill orders on the same side of the market. They will purchase when they believe that an imbalance of buy orders over sell orders will push the market up and sell when they believe the opposite. Their order anticipation strategies try to identify predictable patterns in order submission. They may search for patterns in order submissions, trades, or the relations between trades and other events.

In most jurisdictions, dealers and brokers cannot legally front-run orders that their clients have submitted. These orders include large orders that they know their clients are breaking up to fill in small pieces. But dealers and brokers can study records of their clients' past orders in an attempt to predict orders not yet submitted. They may trade on patterns they identify in orders that they have seen.

For example, if dealers serving retail clients recognize that their clients are predominantly buying, the dealers can buy for their own accounts. If the expected purchase orders materialize—as they often do because many retail clients react to the same stimuli—the dealers may profit by selling to their clients at a higher price. Dealers may justify this practice by claiming that when they first recognize their clients' needs, they actively collect inventory to satisfy those needs and, in particular, acquire market liquidity on behalf of their clients that other traders otherwise might have taken. This argument would be more palatable if the dealers provided better prices to their clients as a result of their early trading. However, because dealers generally fill small customer orders at the market prices that prevail when they receive the orders—prices that may be higher because of the dealers' front running—the small traders likely do not benefit from the dealers' front running.

Some dealers and brokers do not use past order histories to predict future orders because their customers do not approve of the practice. Because most customers are unaware of the practice, however, some broker-dealers probably engage in this type of legal, if perhaps ethically challenged, front running. The benefits associated with the front running of anticipated orders based on knowledge of past orders give a competitive advantage to those dealers and brokers who are willing to engage in this activity (assuming that their clients do not know about it). This competitive advantage is problematic for those brokers and dealers who believe that this type of trading is improper and thus refuse to engage in it.

Regulators could try to make this type of electronic front running illegal by prohibiting electronic traders from accessing information about previous orders. However, such a prohibition could never be applied to manual dealers who have always been aware of the future implications of the past orders they have seen. Therefore, a prohibition of this type of electronic front running would be effective only to the extent that electronic dealing is otherwise more efficient than manual dealing. If such a regulation were promulgated and if the benefits of front running anticipated client orders were sufficiently great, dealers would switch from electronic trading systems to manual systems.

Some front runners also look for patterns in executed trades. For example, suppose that a trader sees that trades of a given size have been occurring at the offer every 10 minutes for an hour. If the trader has seen this pattern of trading before, the trader may suspect that the activity will continue. If so, the trader may buy on the assumption that a trader is in the market filling a large buy order by breaking it into smaller pieces.

Buy-side traders, and the brokers who provide them with algorithms to manage large orders, are aware of the efforts that electronic traders make to detect and front-run their orders. Accordingly, they randomize their strategies to make them more difficult to detect. They submit orders at random times instead of at regular intervals, and they submit various sizes instead of the same size.[10] Although these techniques make detection more difficult, hiding large liquidity-demanding trades is always difficult because sophisticated traders can ultimately identify them by the inevitable relation between prices and volumes that they create. Electronic front runners look for these patterns, often using very advanced automated data-mining tools.

Finally, some front runners examine the relation between trades and other events to predict future trades. For example, when Jim Cramer says on his *Mad Money* television show that he is bullish on a stock, the markets often receive a small surge of retail buy orders in that stock. Traders who identify these events quickly may be able to profit by buying ahead of the retail traders. Because many retail and institutional traders initiate trades in response to common stimuli or in response to predictable situations, traders who can identify patterns in the relations between trades and events may profit from trading ahead. When the time between the stimulus and the response is short, electronic traders have a clear advantage.

*Electronic quote matchers* try to exploit the option values of standing orders. Options to trade are valuable to quote matchers because they allow them to take positions with potentially limited losses. Quote matchers buy when they believe they can rely on standing buy orders to get out of their positions, and they sell when they can do the same with standing sell orders. Traders say that quote matchers lean on these orders. If prices then move in the quote matchers' favor, they profit for as long as they stay in the security or contract. But if the quote matchers conclude that prices are moving against them, they immediately try to exit by trading with the standing orders and thereby limiting their losses.

For example, a fast quote matcher may buy when a slow trader is bidding at 20. If the price subsequently rises, the quote matcher will profit. If the

---

[10]The cat-and-mouse game played by algorithm authors and front runners can become quite sophisticated. For example, researchers have studied the distribution of trade times across milliseconds within a second in US stock data. Interestingly, the distribution they found is not uniform, as one might expect if order submission times were approximately random. Instead, trades were more common early in the one-second interval (peaking about 15–20 milliseconds after the beginning of the interval) than later within the interval. This pattern was undoubtedly due to electronic trading systems' timing their order submissions. Although the algorithm authors may have randomized their submission times down to the second, they apparently did not randomize down to the millisecond. Note that this pattern can be observed only if many electronic trading systems have synchronized their computers' clocks to the same time standard (provided by internet time services using atomic clocks). US regulators require such synchronization to ensure that audit trails are meaningful. Once the pattern became well known, algorithm authors very likely updated their codes to eliminate the pattern.

**45**

quote matcher believes that the price will fall, the quote matcher will sell the position to the buyer at 20 and thereby limit his losses.

The main risk of the quote-matching strategy is that the standing order may be unavailable when the quote matcher needs it. Standing orders disappear when filled by another trader or when canceled.

Quote matchers thus need to estimate the probabilities that standing orders will continue to stand. To that end, they may study orders to see what happens to them. For example, orders that have been standing for a few minutes are more likely to continue to stand for the next 15 seconds than orders that were just submitted. And orders placed behind many other orders at the same price will likely stand longer than orders at the top of the queue.

Quote matchers also need to estimate the probabilities that prices will move to their advantage. They may consider what orders are standing on the other side of the market, how large they are, and how long ago they were submitted.

Quote matchers combine these two types of information, and more, to determine when quote matching may be profitable. Those traders who can analyze standing orders better than others have the best chance of profiting from this strategy.

After quote matchers have established their positions, they must monitor them very closely. In particular, they must continuously consider whether to close their positions. If the orders on which they are relying to protect their positions are canceled or filled and if their trades have not yet proved profitable, quote matchers will usually try to quickly exit their positions. If their trades prove profitable, the option values provided by the standing quotes on which the quote matchers rely will diminish as the price change causes them to go out of the money. If no new orders have been submitted that provide protection closer to current prices, quote matchers will likely close their positions because they will have successfully achieved the premise of their trade—exploiting order option values—and they can extract little further value from the original standing orders.

**Buy-Side Traders.** Most large buy-side traders use electronic order management systems (OMSs) to manage their trading. These systems keep track of the orders that their portfolio managers want filled, which orders have been sent out to be filled, and which fills have already been obtained. Buy-side OMSs generally allow the buy-side trader to route orders to various entities for further handling, along with instructions for how they should be handled. These entities may include brokers, dealers, various alternative trading systems, and in some cases, exchanges. The OMSs typically have dashboards that allow the buy-side trader to see summaries of all activity of interest so that the trader can better manage the trading process. Finally, the OMSs help the buy-side traders report and confirm the trades to all interested parties.

**Electronic Buy-Side Brokers.** Buy-side traders often employ electronic brokers to arrange their trades. In addition to supporting standard order instructions, such as limit or market orders, these brokers often provide a full suite of advanced orders, trading tactics, and algorithms. The broker's electronic trading system generally manages these advanced orders, tactics, and algorithms, but in some cases, exchanges may perform these functions.

■ *Advanced order types.* Advanced orders generally are limit orders with limit prices that change as market conditions change. An example would be a *pegged limit order* for which the trader would like to maintain a bid or an offer at a particular distance relative to some benchmark. Suppose that a trader wants to peg a limit buy order two ticks below the current ask. A broker who supports this instruction may forward it to an exchange that supports the instruction if the probability of the order's filling at that exchange is favorable compared with other exchanges. Otherwise, the broker's computer will manage the order by submitting a limit order priced two ticks below the current ask. When the ask rises or falls, the exchange system will immediately cancel the order and replace it with a new limit order to keep the order at two ticks below the current ask. Effective management of a pegged limit order requires an electronic trading system with very low latency. If the order is not adjusted quickly enough, it risks being executed at an unfavorable price (in this example, if prices drop) or being resubmitted after other orders have been placed at the new price so the probability of execution at that price will be lower (if prices rise). Traders sometimes call pegged limit orders floating limit orders.

■ *Trading tactics.* A trading tactic is a plan for executing a simple function that generally involves the submission of multiple orders. Note that the distinction between advanced orders and tactics can be arbitrary, and not all traders will use the same language to describe various trading functions.

An example of a trading tactic is an instruction to sweep through every market at a given price in an effort to find hidden trading opportunities. Suppose that the best exposed bid among all trading venues is 20.00 and the best exposed offer is 20.02. Because many trading systems permit traders to hide their orders, hidden buyers or sellers may be willing to trade at the 20.01 midpoint. Depending on the exchange, at least three types of orders could permit a trade at the midpoint. First, among exchanges that permit hidden orders, one or more exchanges may be holding a hidden limit order at 20.01.

Second, among exchanges that permit discretionary limit orders, one or more exchanges may be holding a discretionary limit order that can be filled at the midpoint. For example, suppose that an exchange is holding a limit order to buy at 19.99 with 0.02 discretion. This order can be filled at 20.01 if a suitable sell limit order arrives at that price. Finally, among exchanges and dark pools (described in Section 6.6) that permit midspread orders, one or more exchanges or dark pools may be holding such an order. A midspread order is a limit order that is pegged to the midpoint of the quoted bid–ask spread.

To find such hidden liquidity, an electronic trading system may submit an immediate-or-cancel limit order priced at 20.01 to the exchange that the trader expects will most likely have hidden liquidity on the needed side of the market. If such liquidity exists, the order will execute up to the minimum of the sizes of the two orders. If not, the exchange will immediately cancel the order and report the cancellation. If the order has any remaining unfilled size, the electronic trading system will search for liquidity at another exchange. This process will continue until the order is filled or until the trader decides that further search is probably futile.

This sweeping tactic is most effective when the electronic trading system managing it has very low latency. A slow system may lose an opportunity to trade if someone else takes it first. Also, a slow system that obtains one or more partial fills may lose opportunities to trade at other exchanges if the proprietary electronic trading systems managing those opportunities cancel their standing orders when they suspect someone is sweeping the market, as they might if they see trade reports inside the quoted spread.

An example of another trading tactic is placing a limit order at some price with the hope that it will fill at that price. If the order does not fill after some time period (which might be random or based on information), the electronic trading system will cancel the order and resubmit it with an improved price (a higher price for a buy order or a lower price for a sell order). The process is repeated until the order fills.

■ *Algorithms.* Algorithms ("algos" for short) are programmed strategies for filling orders. Algorithms may use combinations or sequences of simple orders, advanced orders, or trading tactics to achieve their objectives. For example, a simple algorithm designed to fill market buy orders in securities with wide bid–ask spreads might sweep the entire market, using the sweep tactic previously described, at successively higher prices until the order is filled.

Many algorithms break up large orders and submit the pieces to various markets over time. Breaking up orders makes it difficult for other traders to infer that a trader is trying to fill a large order. The algorithms typically submit the orders at random times, in random sizes, and sometimes to randomly selected exchanges to hide their common origin.

The rates at which algorithms try to fill large orders may depend on market volumes or on elapsed time. For example, VWAP algorithms attempt to obtain a volume-weighted average fill price that is close to (or better than) the volume-weighted average price (VWAP) of all trades arranged within a prespecified time interval. To minimize the variation between the actual average fill price and the VWAP over the interval, these algorithms try to participate in an equal fraction of all trading volume throughout the interval. To do so, the algorithm must forecast the total expected trading volume in the interval. For example, if the order is for 100,000 shares to be executed over a full trading day and the algorithm expects that trading volume will be 1,000,000 shares for the day, the algorithm will try to participate in 10% of all trades throughout the day. In practice, the execution rate will vary because volumes will differ from expectations. The algorithm thus must periodically adjust its trading plan to obtain the VWAP price it seeks. Buy-side traders use VWAP algorithms when obtaining the average market price within an interval is acceptable to them or their portfolio managers.

Many algorithms use floating limit orders with the hope of obtaining cheap executions. If they fail to fill after some time period, they may switch to more aggressively priced orders or to marketable orders to ensure that they fill.

Large traders who use algorithms to manage their orders are especially concerned about hiding their intentions from front runners. Many electronic traders use artificial intelligence systems to detect when large traders are present in the market. In particular, they look for patterns that large traders may leave. For example, a poorly designed algorithm may submit orders exactly at the same millisecond within a second whenever it submits an order. A clever trader who is aware of this regularity may detect when a large trader is in the market and, equally important, when the trader has completed filling his order. To avoid these problems, algorithm designers often randomize order submission times and sizes to avoid producing patterns that might give them away. They also sometimes try to hide their orders among other orders so that front runners cannot easily identify their intentions.

Developing good algorithms requires extensive research into the origins of transaction costs. Algorithm authors must understand transaction costs well so that they can design algorithms that will trade effectively. To that end, algorithm providers build and estimate models of the costs of trading orders of various sizes, models of the impact trades of a given size or frequency will have on prices, and models of the probabilities that limit orders will fill under a variety of conditions. They must also predict volumes accurately. The most effective algorithms are based on the best research and implemented on the fastest and most capable electronic systems.

Good algorithms generally obtain low-cost executions by knowing when and where to offer liquidity via limit orders, when to use market orders, and how to most effectively keep the market from being aware of their efforts. They reduce the price impacts of large trades.

**Some Observations about Electronic Trading.** This subsection provides some observations about characteristics of electronic trading.

■ *Hidden orders.* Hidden orders are very common in electronic markets. Traders—especially large traders—submit them when they do not want to reveal the existence of the trading options that their standing orders provide to the markets. Traders concerned about quote matchers can protect themselves to some extent by submitting hidden limit orders. Note that hidden limit orders are the electronic equivalent of giving orders to floor brokers to fill with the understanding that the floor brokers may expose the orders only if they can arrange trades. Such orders work better at electronic exchanges than at floor-based exchanges because computers never inadvertently or intentionally display these orders improperly.

In electronic markets, the most common type of order by far is the immediate-or-cancel (IOC) limit order. Traders use these orders to discover hidden orders without revealing their trading intentions. Because they cancel immediately if they do not find liquidity, these orders are also hidden.

Some electronic traders try to discover hidden orders by *pinging* the market. To do so, they submit a small IOC limit order for only a few shares at the price at which they are looking for hidden orders. If the pinging order trades, they know that a hidden order is present at that price, but they do not know the full size of the order (which they can discover only by trading with it). On the basis of this information, traders may adjust their trading strategies.

For example, suppose that a trader wants to buy when the displayed market is 20 bid, offered at 24. The trader might want to place a buy order at 21, but doing so may not be the best strategy if a hidden bid is in the market at 22. The trader could discover whether a hidden bid is in the market by submitting a very small IOC limit order to buy at 22. If this pinging order does not fill, the trader may choose to submit a limit buy order at 21 and perhaps hide it. But if the pinging order fills, the trader may choose to submit a displayed limit buy order at 22, which at most markets would have precedence over the hidden order at 22 because it is displayed.

Quote matchers also may want to ping markets to discover whether they can rely on hidden liquidity to protect their positions. If the ping finds hidden liquidity, they may choose to hold their positions open longer than if the ping finds no hidden liquidity.

All traders who subscribe to a complete trade feed that includes odd-lot transactions can see the results of a ping that discovers liquidity. At almost all exchanges, however, only the pinger will know on which side of the market the hidden liquidity lies. Nonetheless, the information produced by someone else's successful ping can be useful to various traders. It indicates that someone in the market is concerned enough about liquidity conditions that pinging is worthwhile and that hidden liquidity is available on one side of the market.

Buy-side traders can protect themselves from giving up information to pingers by placing minimum fill size instructions on their orders at those exchanges that support such instructions. Depending on the exchange, however, such instructions may lower the trader's order precedence if another limit order without this restriction is at the same price, an unlikely occurrence when the order is priced inside the spread.

■ *Leapfrog.* When spreads are wide, dealers are often willing to trade at better prices than they quote. They quote wide spreads because they hope to trade at more favorable prices. When another trader quotes a better price, dealers often immediately quote an even better price. For example, if the market is 20 bid, offered at 28, and a buy-side trader bids at 21, a dealer might instantly bid at 22. (The improved price might also come from a quote matcher.) This behavior generally frustrates buy-side traders, who must then quote a better price to maintain order precedence. If the spread is sufficiently wide, a game of leapfrog may ensue as the dealer jumps ahead again. As an alternative, when confronted with this situation, the buy-side trader could submit a hidden bid at 21.

■ *Flickering quotes.* Electronic markets often have flickering quotes, which are exposed limit orders that electronic traders submit and then cancel shortly thereafter, often within a second. Electronic dealers and algorithmic buy-side traders submit and repeatedly cancel and resubmit their orders when they do not want their orders to stand in the market but they do want other traders to see that they are willing to trade at the displayed price.

Some manual buy-side traders complain about flickering quotes because they cannot take them before they disappear. These traders can trade with a flickering quote by submitting hidden limit orders priced where they think a flickering quote will reappear. If the quote reappears at that price, the buy-side trader will immediately trade.

■ *Machine learning.* Machine learning, also known as data mining, uses advanced statistical methods to characterize data structures, particularly relations among variables. These methods include neural nets, genetic algorithms, classifiers, and other methods designed to explain variables of interest using sparse data or data for which the number of potential explanatory variables far exceeds the number of observations.

Machine-learning methods produce models based on observed empirical regularities rather than on theoretical principles identified by analysts. These methods can be very powerful when vast amounts of data are generated from stable processes.

Many trading problems are ideally suited for machine-learning analyses because the problems repeat regularly and often. For such problems, machine-based learning systems can be extraordinarily powerful.

However, these systems are often useless—or worse—when trading becomes extraordinary, as when volatilities shoot up. Machine-learning systems frequently do not produce useful information during volatility episodes because they have few precedents from which the machines can learn. Thus, traders often instruct their electronic trading systems to stop trading—and sometimes to close out their positions—whenever they recognize that they are entering uncharted territory. Many traders shut down when volatility spikes, both because high-volatility episodes are uncommon and thus not well understood and because even if such episodes were well understood, they represent periods of exceptionally high risk.

## 5.3. The Three Needs for Speed

Electronic traders must be fast to trade effectively, regardless of whether they are proprietary traders or buy-side traders. Electronic traders have three needs for speed:

1.  *Taking.* Electronic traders sometimes want to take a trading opportunity before others do. A new trading opportunity may attract many traders, and an existing trading opportunity may attract many traders when market events cause it to become more valuable (e.g., a standing limit order to sell becomes much more attractive when the prices of correlated securities rise). Often only the first trader to reach the attractive opportunity will be able to benefit. Thus, electronic traders must be fast so they can beat other traders to take attractive trading opportunities.

2.  *Making.* Market events often create attractive opportunities to offer liquidity. For example, at most exchanges when prices rise, the first traders to place bids at improved prices acquire time precedence at those prices that may allow them to trade sooner or at better prices than they otherwise would be able to trade. Therefore, electronic traders must be fast so they can acquire precedence when they want it before other traders do.

3. *Canceling.* Frequently, traders must quickly cancel orders they no longer want to fill, often because market events have increased the option value of those orders. For example, if traders have limit buy orders standing at the best bid and large trades take place at other exchanges at the same price, these traders may reasonably conclude that prices may drop and that they may obtain better executions at a lower price. They must cancel their orders as quickly as possible to reduce the probability that they will trade. As a general rule, trading when you do not want to trade is unprofitable.

Traders sometimes cancel their orders when one of their standing limit orders fills. For example, suppose that a trader has placed standing limit orders to buy two closely correlated stocks, such as IBM and Oracle. These stocks are correlated because both companies are in the business information services industry. If the IBM order fills, the trader may cancel the Oracle order simply because the trader does not want too much exposure to common risks associated with the industry. The trader must cancel the order quickly because other traders may try to sell Oracle if they believe that the values of all companies in that industry have fallen. Such traders may include electronic pairs traders or news traders.

**Only Comparative Advantage Matters.** Note that electronic traders do not simply need to be fast to trade effectively—they must be *faster* than their competitors. Little inherent value comes from being fast. The value lies in being faster. The reason electronic trading systems have such low latencies (i.e., are incredibly fast) is that electronic traders have been trying for years to be faster than their competitors.

Electronic order-handling systems used by exchanges also have grown faster as exchanges compete for the order flows from electronic traders. Electronic traders often will not send orders to exchanges where they cannot quickly cancel them, especially if other exchanges have faster systems. Accordingly, exchanges with slow order-handling systems have lost market share.

The adoption of Regulation NMS (National Market System) by the SEC effectively forced all US exchanges to use electronic order execution systems. Following this adoption, the New York Stock Exchange's electronic markets were slow compared with those of its competitors, particularly such new alternative trading systems as BATS and Direct Edge, which have since registered as exchanges. As a result, the market share of the NYSE in its listed stocks fell from 80% to 20%. The NYSE has since changed its rules and improved its electronic systems to become more competitive, but the damage was done, and it has not recovered its former market share.

## 5.4.   How to Trade Quickly

*Latency* is the elapsed time between the occurrence of an event and an action that depends on that event. For example, the event might be a trade at one exchange and the action might be the receipt by another exchange of an instruction to cancel a standing order that a trader has sent upon learning of the trade. Electronic traders measure these latencies in milliseconds or microseconds (millionths of a second).

The latency of a linear multi-step process is the sum of the latencies of each step in the process. The submission of an order instruction by a trader in response to an event consists of three major steps, each of which involves many smaller steps beyond the scope of this discussion:

1.   The trader must learn that the event took place.

2.   The trader must respond to the new information with a new order instruction.

3.   The trader must send, and the exchange must receive, the new instruction.

Traders must use very fast communication systems to minimize the latencies associated with steps 1 and 3 (communicating in and out), and they must use very fast computer systems to minimize the latency associated with step 2 (responding).

**Fast Communications.** Electronic traders and brokers use several strategies to minimize their communication times. These strategies involve minimizing communication distances and maximizing line speeds.

Note that the relevant measure of communication distance is the total of two distances that signals must travel. The first distance is from where the event is reported (often an exchange but sometimes another type of news source) to the computer that will process the information. The second distance is from the computer to the exchange trading system where the trader wants to deliver an order instruction.

Electronic traders and brokers locate their computers as close as possible to the exchanges at which they trade to minimize latencies due to physics: No message can travel faster than the speed of light. At 300,000 kilometers (186,000 miles) per second in a vacuum, light travels only 300 kilometers in a millisecond. Although the speed of light is incredibly fast, note that a fast computer with a clock speed of 5 GHz (billion cycles per second) can do 5 million operations in a millisecond, which is usually much more than required to receive information, process it, and send out an instruction in response.

Communication latencies are particularly important when messages must travel significant distances. For example, the great circle (shortest) distances between Chicago and New York and between New York and London are, respectively, 1,146 kilometers and 5,576 kilometers. Thus, round-trip communications between these two pairs of cities have minimum latencies of approximately 8 and 37 milliseconds simply because of the speed of light. (The actual minimum latencies are longer because the speed of light in standard optical fiber is 31% slower than the speed of light in a vacuum.) Such delays illustrate that no electronic trader located at any significant distance from where information is created or must be delivered can effectively compete with traders who have minimized these combined distances.

Many exchanges allow electronic traders to place their servers in the rooms where the exchange servers operate, a practice called *collocation*. Exchanges charge substantial fees for collocation space and related services such as air conditioning and power. Note that even within collocation centers, concerns about fairness dictate that the communication lines connecting proprietary servers to exchange servers all be of the same length for all customers buying the same class of collocation service. During the time it takes for light to travel 10 meters, a 5 GHz computer can do 167 operations.

Electronic traders and brokers also use the fastest communication technologies they can obtain to collect and transmit information when any distance separates the places where information events occur from the places where they act on those events. To that end, they use the fastest and most direct communication lines that are available. For example, they prefer line-of-sight microwave channels to fiber-optic and copper channels because of the differences in speed of electromagnetic wave propagation through these materials. (Microwaves travel through air at just slightly below the speed of light, whereas signals travel through fiber-optic channels and copper wires only two-thirds as quickly.) They also ensure that their communications pass through the fewest electronic routers and switches possible because passage through each of these devices adds its own latency to the total latency of the line.

Finally, electronic traders and brokers subscribe to special high-speed data feeds directly from exchanges and other data vendors. The vendors charge premium prices for these services, which are delivered over very high-speed communication lines. Some exchanges provide multiple classes of data services that vary by speed to price-discriminate among their clients.

**Fast Computations.** Once electronic traders receive information about an event of interest, they must decide whether to act on that information and how. Those traders who can make decisions faster than their competitors will trade more profitably. Electronic traders minimize the latencies associated with their decision making by using several strategies.

First and most obviously, they use very fast computers. They overclock their processors (run them faster than the processor designers intended) and use liquid cooling systems to keep them from melting. They store all information in fast memory to avoid the latencies associated with physical disk drives, which cannot deliver information while their heads are seeking the right track and which can deliver information only as fast as their disks spin once the right track is found. They sometimes use specialized processors designed to quickly solve their specific trading problems, and they may even use processors etched on gallium arsenide rather than silicon.

Electronic traders also must run very efficient software. They often use simple and specialized operating systems to avoid the overhead associated with supporting operating system functions they do not use. Remarkably, many electronic trading systems run under variants of the original MS-DOS operating system because of its simplicity.

Electronic traders optimize their computer code for speed. They often write important functions that they use repeatedly in assembler language to ensure that they run quickly. (Code written in high-level languages, such as C++, tends to be slower because their compilers are designed to handle all types of code, not just code written to solve trading problems.) And they avoid using languages such as Python because they are interpreter languages that compile (create executable machine code) as they run, rather than compile when first written.

Some electronic trading problems change so frequently that speed of coding is more important than speed of execution. For example, some problems depend on ever-changing sets of exceptions or opportunities. For such problems, traders use high-level languages (e.g., Python), because they can code faster and more accurately in these languages than in lower-level languages, such as C++. If they expect that the software will remain useful, they may later recode their routines in other languages to make them run faster.

Some electronic traders also reduce latency by creating contingency tables that contain prearranged action plans. For example, suppose that a bid rises in a market in which electronic traders are active. In response to the increased bid, traders may want to raise their bids or offers. The decision to do so may depend on their inventory positions and perhaps on many other factors as well. To decide what to do following an increased bid may require substantial analyses, which take time. Traders can reduce their decision latencies by doing these analyses before the bid increases instead of afterward. Seeing the increased bid, they can respond by simply looking up the optimal response in a contingency table stored in memory. To be useful, the contingency tables must be kept up to date, and they must provide responses for most likely events. In this example, traders presumably would also have precomputed responses for a decrease in bid, among many other contingencies.

## 5.5. Why Computers Win

Computers have come to dominate the implementation of many trading strategies because they are so efficient and so unlike human traders.

- Computers have infinite attention spans. The scope of their attention also can be very wide. They can continuously watch and respond to information from many instruments and many markets simultaneously and essentially forever.

- Their responses are extraordinarily fast.

- Computers are perfectly disciplined. They do only what they are instructed to do.

- Computers also do not forget any information that their programmers want to save.

- Finally, computers do not argue about office assignments, sulk about pay, or harass their assistants.

The efficiency of electronic trading strategies led to their widespread adoption by proprietary traders, buy-side traders, and brokers. Electronic traders have displaced traditional dealers, arbitrageurs, and brokers in almost all electronic markets.

## 5.6. Effects on Transaction Costs

Numerous studies show that transaction costs declined with the growth of electronic trading over time. Some studies also show that at a given point in time, lower transaction costs are found in those markets with the greatest intensity of electronic trading. These time-series and cross-sectional results are not surprising. They are due to the greater cost efficiencies associated with electronic trading.

With the growth of electronic trading, bid–ask spreads decreased substantially. These decreases lowered transaction costs for retail traders and for institutions trading small orders.

Overall transaction costs also decreased for large orders, many of which are now broken into smaller parts for execution. A study of the execution costs of tens of thousands of equity orders for US stocks involving tens of millions of dollars of principal value shows that the implementation shortfall cost of filling those orders dropped with the growth of electronic trading. This evidence suggests that any profits obtained by parasitic traders from front running orders are smaller than the cost savings obtained by buy-side traders from trading in electronic markets using algorithms.

# 6. Practitioner and Regulatory Issues Associated with Fast Electronic Markets

This chapter addresses nine issues associated with fast electronic markets that concern practitioners and regulators. The issues appear in order of descending generality. The first issues (Sections 6.1–6.4) concern broad questions of economic efficiency, fairness, and systemic risk; the middle issues (Sections 6.5–6.7) concern the competition among exchange service providers (exchanges and dark pools); and the last issues (Sections 6.8 and 6.9) concern rules that affect transaction costs incurred by buy-side traders.

## 6.1. Does Speed Help Capital Formation?

Because no one makes capital allocation decisions in milliseconds, many people ask, What is the benefit of having markets that operate at such high speeds? In particular, would economies be worse off if markets were not so fast? The simple answer to this question is a nuanced *no*—but the nuance is important.

Economic efficiency in market-based economies requires informative prices to help ensure that companies, governments, and people use resources where they are most valuable. Among these resources are new capital for investment and skilled managers to manage existing capital investments. In primary (new-issue) security markets, informative prices ensure that only the best ideas get new capital. In secondary security markets, informative prices help ensure that only the best managers manage existing projects. Both conditions are essential for economic efficiency.

Prices are most informative in liquid markets in which informed traders can arrange their trades without much impact on price. In such markets, informed trading is profitable and many informed traders compete to acquire and analyze information. If slower markets could produce equally informative prices, slowing markets would not impair economic efficiency.

Now consider the nuance. Electronic trading substantially reduced transaction costs, and so markets are now more liquid than before. The additional liquidity has undoubtedly produced more informative prices, although empirical documentation of any improvements is difficult because "true" values are never observed.[11]

---

[11]Some tangential evidence suggests that markets are indeed more informative. In particular, price change serial correlations over short intervals are now closer to zero than before, which suggests that prices more closely follow the random walk expected of highly informative prices. However, this evidence is also consistent with a reduction in transaction costs.

By making investing less costly, electronic trading may also have increased total funds available for investment, which in principle should have decreased capital-raising costs for issuers in the primary security markets. This conclusion is less certain because investors who fear electronic trading may shy away from the markets. The net effect on total investable funds depends on whether investors value the increased liquidity more than they fear electronic trading. In any event, empirical documentation of any effect that fast markets have had on investment funds is nearly impossible because so many other factors also affect investment decisions.

Overall, the adoption of electronic trading systems probably improved economic efficiency because it led to more informative prices, greater liquidity, and perhaps more investment due to fewer frictions.

These efficiencies are attributable to the automation of trading and not to the speed at which trading takes place. In principle, if markets remained automated but were somehow slowed, the benefits to economic efficiency might be preserved. If regulators ever attempt to slow the markets, however, they must take care to ensure that they do not increase transaction costs in the process.

Markets now are fast because electronic traders compete with each other to be the fastest traders and because electronic exchanges compete with each other to attract electronic traders. These competitions greatly reduced latencies and coincidently reduced transaction costs compared with manual trading systems as high-frequency dealers and arbitrageurs displaced manual traders.

## 6.2. The HFT Arms Race

The competition among high-frequency traders has created an arms race in which each trader tries to be faster than the next. As a consequence, high-frequency-trading technologies are now very expensive, making entry quite costly.

These barriers to entry can create natural monopolies. Although substantial evidence suggests that electronic trading benefits the markets, these benefits may erode if only a few HFTs survive and are able to exploit their unique positions. Already, many HFTs are quitting the markets because they cannot compete effectively.

More generally, many commentators have observed that most of the costs of high-frequency trading do little to promote better or more liquid markets. HFTs primarily incur costs so they can beat their competitors. Thus, these costs are wasted costs of competition that utilitarian traders must ultimately bear.

These concerns have led to calls for changes in market structure that would diminish the advantages of being faster. Some commentators suggest that markets be slowed by running call markets once a second or more often instead of trading continuously. Others suggest that the order processing be delayed by random intervals to reduce the benefits of being fast and thus the incentives to invest in speed.

## 6.3. Is Electronic Trading Fair?

Many traders believe that high-speed markets are unfair because electronic traders can see and react to more information—and sooner—than can manual traders. Whether or not this advantage is fair depends on the values of the observer. Not surprisingly, many slow traders do not think the advantage is fair whereas many electronic traders think otherwise.

Economics cannot resolve this issue—it can only identify implications of various policies. Accordingly, in this discussion I will not opine on the fairness of electronic trading. However, many readers may find it instructive to consider several observations:

- Some traders have always had superior access to markets. For example, floor-based traders saw information and could react to it more quickly than could other traders. This observation does not mean that floor-based trading was fair, but it does indicate that the advent of electronic trading simply redistributed informational advantages.

- Anyone can be fast by investing in the necessary technologies or by trading through a broker who offers fast trading tools. Note, however, that speedy trading technologies can be very expensive.

- Competition among fast traders limits their profits because they compete away the advantages they obtain from their superior efficiency. Some readers may find this observation comforting, but buy-side investors who believe that electronic parasitic traders exploit their orders will find little consolation in it.

## 6.4. Systemic Risks of Electronic Trading

Electronic trading created new systemic risks that concern regulators and practitioners. A *systemic risk* is a risk that some failure will hurt more than just the entity responsible for the failure. Systemic risks are particularly problematic when the responsible entity is not required or is unable to compensate others for the costs its failure imposes on them. When people do not bear the full costs of their behaviors, they tend not to be as careful in avoiding damaging behaviors as they otherwise would be.

Systemic risks associated with fast trading may be due to electronic exchange trading system failures or to excessive orders submitted by electronic traders. Electronic exchange trading system failures occur when programmers make mistakes, exchange servers have insufficient capacity to handle traffic, or computer hardware or communication lines fail.

The 18 May 2012 Facebook IPO at NASDAQ is an example of a trading system failure due to a programming error that unexpectedly high demands on capacity revealed. In this case, two software processes locked into an infinite loop as they took turns responding to each other.

Examples of systemic risks due to excessive orders submitted by electronic traders include the following:

- *Runaway algorithms that produce streams of unintended orders as a result of programming mistakes.* The problems sometimes occur when programmers do not anticipate some contingency. The Knight Capital trading failure on 1 August 2012 may be the most extreme example of a runaway algorithm incident. Owing to a software programming mistake, Knight sent millions of orders to the markets over a 45-minute period when it intended only to fill 212 orders, some of which normally might have been broken up but none of which would have generated so many orders. These orders produced 4 million executions involving 397 stocks. Knight lost $400 million in the incident.

- *Fat finger errors that occur when a manual trader submits a larger order than intended.* They are called fat finger errors because they sometimes occur when a trader hits the wrong key or hits a key more often than intended. These types of errors are not unique to electronic trading systems, but their consequences are often greater in electronic systems because of the speed at which they operate and because in manual trading systems, clerks often catch these errors before they cause problems.

- *Overlarge orders that demand more liquidity than the market can provide.* In these events, a trader—often inexperienced—will try to execute a marketable order that is too large for the market to handle without severely disrupting prices in the time given to fill the order. The 6 May 2010 Flash Crash occurred as a result of such an order. The crash was triggered when a large institutional trader tried to sell $4.1 billion in E-mini S&P 500 futures contracts using an algorithm over a short period of time. The algorithm was designed to participate in a fixed fraction of the market volume. When the initial trades depressed S&P 500 futures prices, trading volumes increased substantially as arbitrageurs and others started to trade. The increase in trading volumes caused the algorithm to increase the rate of its order submissions, which exacerbated the problem. The market reverted to its former levels after the Chicago Mercantile Exchange briefly halted trading in the E-mini S&P 500 futures contract, and the large order was eventually filled. Appendix A provides a fuller discussion of the Flash Crash.

- *Malevolent order streams created deliberately to disrupt the markets.* The perpetrators may be market manipulators; aggrieved employees, such as traders or software engineers; or terrorists. Traders conducting denial-of-service attacks designed to overwhelm their competitors' electronic trading systems with excessive quotes may also create malevolent order streams.

**Solutions to Systemic Risk Problems.** The solutions to the systemic risk problems associated with electronic trading systems are multifold.

- Most obviously, traders must test software thoroughly before using it in real time. Exchanges often conduct mock trading sessions to allow developers to test their software.

- Rigorous market access controls must ensure that only those orders coming from approved sources enter electronic order-matching systems.

- Rigorous access controls on software developers must ensure that only authorized developers can change software. Best practice mandates that these controls also include the requirement that all software be read, understood, and vouched for by at least one developer besides its author.

- The electronic traders who generate orders and the electronic exchanges that receive orders must surveil their order flow in real time to ensure that it conforms to preset parameters that characterize its expected volume, size, and other characteristics. When the order flow is different than expected, automatic controls must shut it off immediately.

- Brokers must surveil all orders that they introduce into electronic trading systems. Brokers must not allow their clients to enter orders directly into exchange trading systems, a process called *naked sponsored access.* Instead, brokers must examine their clients' orders to ensure that their trading is appropriate.

- Some exchanges have adopted price limits and trade halts to stop trading when prices move too quickly. These rules stop trading when excess demands for liquidity occur. They also prevent the extreme price changes that can occur in electronic markets when market orders arrive and no liquidity is present. Some brokers now automatically convert market orders into marketable limit orders to ensure that they do not trade at unreasonable prices.

## 6.5.   Who Owns the Data?

Exchanges earn substantial profits from selling high-speed proprietary data feeds to HFTs. These sales facilitate trading strategies that sometimes disadvantage traders with slower access. Thus, many practitioners and regulators wonder whether exchanges should be allowed to sell proprietary data feeds.

The economics underlying this question are straightforward: The sale of proprietary data allows exchanges to extract some of the profits that HFTs make from orders that other traders send to exchanges. If the exchanges were prohibited from selling the data directly to HFTs, all traders would have to obtain their data from third-party information aggregators, who presumably would be prohibited from creating separate products to favor high-speed traders. Such an arrangement would level the trading playing field, at least with respect to data.

Less clear is the question of whether such arrangements would be fair. The exchanges claim that because they produce the data and because producing data is expensive, they should be entitled to exploit their data as they see fit. In contrast, many buy-side traders believe that they are the ones who actually produce the data through their trading decisions and that the data therefore collectively belong to them. They are offended that they should have to pay so much for the data, especially when they believe that the data, arising from decisions they have made, are being used to hurt them.

## 6.6.   Off-Exchange Trading

In many countries, people can trade stocks away from established exchanges. Dark pools and dealers provide the primary venues for off-exchange trading. Off-exchange trading concerns many practitioners and regulators because it fragments trading, making it more difficult to find liquidity. They also worry that the quality of price discovery may suffer.

**Dark Pools.** *Dark pools* are off-exchange systems that match buyers with sellers. Broker-dealers operate most dark pools—generally as a side business to better serve their brokerage clients, but sometimes as their primary business. Some exchanges and other exchange service vendors also operate dark pools. They are called dark pools because they typically do not display the orders sent to them ("dark") and because they organize liquidity ("pools").

Most dark pools simply match buyers with sellers at the midpoint of the bid–ask spread quoted at other trading venues. Traders using these services send unpriced orders to the dark pool. Practitioners often call such markets *crossing markets* because they cross orders (arrange trades).

Dark pools that organize their trading in call market sessions match buyers with sellers only at the time of the call. Trades are possible only if both buyers and sellers are present in the market. If so, the side with the smaller aggregate size will fill completely, and the orders on the other side will fill partially. Most such systems allocate size to the partially filled side on the basis of pro-rata allocation rules that they write.

Dark pools that organize continuous markets attempt to match orders when they arrive. If an incoming order does not fill immediately, as is typically the case, the pool places the order in its order book to await the arrival of an order on the other side (or cancels the order if it is marked as an IOC order). Some continuous crossing markets trade incoming buy orders at the best offer and incoming sell orders at the best bid (they obtain the best offer and the best bid from other venues).

Crossing markets do not contribute to price discovery because they arrange trades only when both traders are willing to trade at prices obtained from other venues. When the aggregate size of buy orders exceeds that of sell orders, the crossing markets do not raise prices to discourage buyers and encourage sellers. Instead, they simply allocate the scarce sell size to the buy orders according to their trade allocation rules (usually some form of pro-rata allocation).

Some dark pools, such as Liquidnet, facilitate trade negotiation among their clients. Liquidnet's electronic system looks into the electronic order management systems of its buy-side clients to identify the trades that the clients want to arrange. If Liquidnet's trade facilitation system recognizes that two of its clients may be willing to trade with each other, it suggests to them that a trade may be possible and provides a messaging window in which the customers can confidentially negotiate a trade without revealing their orders or their identities to each other or to anyone else. Liquidnet also collects information about how often the customers complete trades with suggested counterparties, and it makes this information available to its clients so that the clients can consider the information when deciding whether to initiate a negotiation.

Dark pools are popular because they allow traders to cheaply arrange trades when willing counterparties are present without participating in the price discovery process, which can be expensive. Large customers like to use dark pools because the systems do not display that they are willing to trade and because the cost of price discovery increases with trade size. The opaqueness of dark pools protects customers from parasitic traders using front-running and quote-matching strategies.

Many dark pools place restrictions on the types of traders who can use their services. Such systems typically try to exclude traders generally known to be well informed (such as hedge funds) because not trading is usually better than trading on the wrong side of the market. In principle, the exclusion of well-informed traders should lower the average transaction costs of less well-informed traders. Such dark pools thus provide a service—protection from informed traders—that exchanges cannot.

**Internalization and Preferencing.** Many dealers who fill retail marketable orders will automatically sell at the best offer or buy at the best bid (or at slightly better prices). They effectively operate continuous crossing markets in which they are the only liquidity suppliers. These dealers, often called *wholesalers*, generally obtain order flows by paying retail brokers to route their customer orders to them. This process is called *preferencing*. If the retail broker routes the orders to its own dealers, the process is called *internalization*.

Payments for order flow depend on how wide bid–ask spreads are and on how well informed the customers are. When spreads are wide and the customers are uninformed, the payments are large because wholesale traders compete to obtain order flows from which they can profit. These payments—and the dealing profits made through internalization—presumably result in lower retail trade commissions and the provision of better ancillary services as retail brokers compete to obtain orders from their clients that they can then sell to wholesalers or internalize. (And more money may be spent on advertising to obtain those order flows.) If the wholesale dealer and retail broker markets are sufficiently competitive and if the retail brokers do not spend too much on advertising, uninformed traders may benefit because the system, in effect, discriminates in their favor by giving them lower net trade costs than they would obtain if they traded at exchanges where bid–ask spreads reflect the adverse selection from better-informed traders.

**Concerns about Off-Exchange Trading.** The growth of dark pools and of internalization and preferencing has raised fears about the quality of the exchange markets. In particular, the removal of order flow from participation in the price discovery process should, in principle, weaken that process and ultimately lead to greater transitory volatility and less informative prices. Not surprisingly, this issue most concerns exchange market operators and the well-informed traders who use exchange markets. The concerns are theoretically well founded, but current evidence does not indicate that the issue is material.

Exchange operators also complain that crossing markets and automated dealers free-ride off data that the exchanges produce. Without such data, traders and brokers would not trust crossing markets and dealers to arrange their trades. Note, however, that the question of who owns data is contentious (discussed in Section 6.5).

The proliferation of off-exchange traders also concerns some practitioners and regulators, who worry that traders cannot easily find liquidity when it is spread over many different venues. These concerns are real, but the problem is self-correcting if no agency problems affect where brokers route orders. As traders learn that some venues are less liquid than others, they will shun the less liquid venues, which will eventually fail.

This solution to the proliferation-of-venues problem works only when brokers faithfully route limit orders to the venues where they will most likely execute and marketable orders to the venues where they will most likely obtain the best prices. If they route orders only to their own venues or to those of their correspondents, their customers' limit orders may execute later than they should, if at all, and their marketable orders may execute at inferior prices. Buy-side traders must ensure that their brokers' routing decisions best serve them and not their brokers.

Despite their opacity, dark pools can leak information. Some leaks are intentional and have led to prosecutions and other regulatory actions. But some clever trading strategies can discover information in dark pools. For example, a trader can discover the heavy side in a crossing market call by submitting a small order. If the order fills completely, the other side is the heavier side. If the order fills only partially, the trader may be able to infer from the total size of the cross how much additional size is on the same side of the market. Crossing markets can control these leaks by requiring minimum order sizes or through the design of their pro-rata allocation schemes.

Because crossing markets use prices derived from other venues, crossing markets are vulnerable to price manipulation. For example, if a clever trader is aware that a large sell order is waiting to fill in a crossing market, the trader may push prices down in the markets where the crossing market obtains its prices by submitting sell orders to those markets. The clever trader will then submit a large buy order to the crossing market, where it may fill at an artificially depressed price. Thus, buy-side traders using crossing markets must be careful not to inadvertently allow information about their orders to slip out.

## 6.7. Maker-Taker Pricing

*Maker-taker pricing* refers to a pricing model that some electronic exchanges use to price their order-matching services. Under this system, the exchange charges a high fee—called the *access fee* or *maker fee*—to the *taker*, the trader who initiates the trade. The exchange then rebates a substantial portion of the fee to the *maker*, who posted the standing limit order that provided the taker with the option to trade. This rebate is called the *liquidity rebate*. Note that maker-taker pricing does not depend on whether the buyer or the seller is the maker or the taker.

For example, at the maker-taker BATS BZX exchange, the standard rate for taking liquidity (the access fee) is $0.003 (0.3¢) per share and the associated rebate rate for adding liquidity is $0.002, so the exchange makes $0.001 per share traded. If Thomas uses a marketable order for 1,000 shares to take a market made by Maria, who placed a standing limit order for 1,500 shares, Thomas will pay an access fee of $3 to the exchange and Maria will receive a rebate of $2. The difference—$1, or 0.1¢ per share—is the net revenue collected by the exchange. Although these fees are quite small, they add up to significant sums when aggregated over billions of traded shares.

In contrast, exchanges that use the traditional pricing model simply charge a small commission for arranging trades. Depending on the exchange, the seller pays, or both the seller and the buyer pay, the exchange fee. Many exchanges—especially futures exchanges—throughout the world still use this traditional pricing model.

Maker-taker pricing and its related converse, taker-maker pricing, have become quite important in many markets, especially in the US equity markets. Analysts must be familiar with this pricing system to understand and control certain agency problems that it facilitates. These problems are best understood through a quick discussion of the origins of maker-taker pricing.

**The Agency Problem Associated with Maker-Taker Pricing.** Maker-taker pricing emerged in the 1990s in the United States when new electronic order-matching systems started to compete with such traditional equity exchanges as the New York Stock Exchange. These systems, known as alternative trading systems (ATSs) or as electronic communications networks (ECNs), initially were unable to garner much order flow. Although many buy-side traders enthusiastically supported their formation, few would use them when they needed to trade. If they wanted to fill marketable orders, they sent them to the established exchanges, where other traders were posting limit orders. And if they wanted to post limit orders, they also sent them to established exchanges because limit orders fill faster at the exchanges where people send market orders. As a consequence, these new electronic trading systems had little liquidity: Few traders would send them market orders because few traders would send them limit orders because few traders would send them market orders—forming a vicious cycle.

Academics call this circularity the *order flow externality problem*. Practitioners simply know it by the principle that "liquidity attracts liquidity." The order flow externality arises because no one directly compensates the traders who post limit orders for the valuable trading options they provide to other traders. (They obtain better prices if they trade, but they often do not trade and most especially do not trade when quote matchers trade to extract the option values of their orders, as described in Section 2.6.) Liquidity attracts liquidity because these free options attract traders. The same principle explains why a crowd forms when a supermarket clerk gives out free cheese samples.

To address this problem, the ECNs created a new pricing system, now called maker-taker pricing. The benefit to these systems from using the maker-taker pricing model comes from the fact that most institutional and retail traders do not pay the exchange access fees or receive the liquidity rebates. Instead, their brokers pay or collect these fees. The liquidity rebates offered by the newly emerging electronic trading systems encouraged brokers to route their customers' standing limit orders to maker-taker exchanges. These orders then made the systems more liquid.

Maker-taker pricing, however, also created an agency problem. Customers whose standing limit orders were routed to maker-taker trading systems were worse off because their orders did not trade as quickly as they would have traded had they been posted at a traditional exchange. To see why, suppose that identical limit 20 sell orders are standing at a traditional exchange and at a maker-taker exchange. All traders willing to buy at 20 will always take the order at the traditional exchange instead of at the maker-taker exchange because the exchange fee at the traditional exchange is small compared with the access fee at the maker-taker exchange. Orders posted at maker-taker exchanges are the last to trade because they are more expensive. If the access fee is $0.003 per share and the traditional fee is $0.0005 per share, the buyer would pay $20.003 per share at the maker-taker exchange instead of $20.0005 per share at the traditional exchange.

The maker-taker pricing system allowed these new electronic exchanges to exploit the agency problem between brokers and their clients. Because most clients, particularly retail clients, were unaware of the routing decisions made by their brokers, nobody complained much. Over time, this agency problem disappeared as almost all US equity exchanges converted to the maker-taker pricing system, with access fees limited by law to $0.003 per share.[12]

---

[12]To attract more order flow, some ECNs raised their access fees to provide higher liquidity rebates. A game of leapfrog resulted as some ECNs tried to maintain the largest liquidity rebates. The SEC's Division of Market Regulation (now called the Division of Trading and Markets) stopped this race through a letter that effectively limited access fees to $0.003/share. This limit was later incorporated into Regulation NMS.

**Equilibrium Effects of Maker-Taker Pricing.** Note that at markets that use maker-taker prices, quoted spreads no longer truly represent the costs of trading. For takers, the true spread is the quoted spread plus twice the access fee. For makers, the true spread is the quoted spread minus twice the liquidity rebate.

Maker-taker pricing undoubtedly decreased average bid–ask spreads in those stocks for which the minimum price variation is not always a binding constraint on quoted spreads. Because the liquidity rebate makes using limit orders more attractive and the access fee makes using market orders less attractive, bid–ask spreads must decrease to ensure that not all traders want to use limit orders when trading. Maker-taker pricing probably decreased average spreads by approximately twice the average of the access fee and the liquidity rebate because this reduction ensured that, all other things being equal, the net spread would be the same before and after the switch to maker-taker pricing. For stocks for which the tick binds bid–ask spreads, maker-taker pricing almost certainly increased displayed quotation sizes as traders competed for liquidity rebates.

Unfortunately, the predicted decreases in spreads and increases in quotation sizes caused by maker-taker pricing cannot be identified easily through empirical studies because too many other factors also affected market spreads and quotation sizes during the period when most exchanges migrated to maker-taker pricing. Some secondary evidence, however, shows that traders consider maker-taker fees when quoting.

**Taker-Maker Pricing.** In the last few years, a few exchange holding companies have introduced new exchanges that use taker-maker pricing instead of maker-taker pricing. Under *taker-maker* pricing, makers pay a positive maker fee and takers receive a rebate when their trades are arranged. For example, the standard rates for adding and removing liquidity at the BATS BYX taker-maker exchange are, respectively, \$0.0018/share and −\$0.0015/share.

Taker-maker pricing cheapens quote-matching strategies by allowing traders to trade at subpenny increments. To see why, suppose that a maker-taker exchange has a substantial aggregate size bid at 10.20 and the best bid at the taker-maker exchange is 10.19. Suppose further that buyer Mike wants to make market but is unwilling to stand in line at 10.20 at the maker-taker exchange. To trade ahead, Mike can go to the taker-maker exchange and bid 10.20. Although the nominal bid matches the best bid at the maker-taker exchange, Mike's bid at the taker-maker exchange will fill first because it offers a higher net price to taking sellers. The net price to the taker at the maker-taker exchange is 10.197 = 10.20 − 0.003, whereas it is 10.2015 = 10.20 − −0.0015 at the taker-maker exchange. The difference is $0.0045/share.

From Mike's point of view as a maker, the 10.20 bid quoted at the maker-taker market implies a post-rebate net price of 10.198 = 10.20 − 0.002. The net price implied at the taker-maker exchange is 10.2015 = 10.20 + 0.0015. The difference of $0.0035/share is Bob's cost of stepping in front of the size at the maker-taker market. Had Bob wanted to trade ahead of the 10.20 bid at the maker-taker exchange, he would have had to bid a full penny higher at 10.21.

The side-by-side operation of maker-taker and taker-maker exchanges effectively reduces the minimum price variation (tick size). Analysts must be aware that quoted bids and offers are not net bids and offers. A 10.20 bid at one exchange does not necessarily represent the same net price at one exchange as it does at another.

The introduction of taker-maker exchanges reestablishes the agency problem first created when maker-taker exchanges started to compete with traditional exchanges. When brokers pay all exchange fees and receive all exchange rebates and maker-taker and taker-maker exchanges are posting the same quote, brokers will always route their customers' standing limit orders to the maker-taker exchanges first and their customers' taking orders to the taker-maker exchanges first. Therefore, customer limit orders may be more susceptible to quote-matching strategies, they may trade later than they otherwise would, or they may fail to trade at all.

In principle, buy-side traders can solve this problem by insisting on paying all exchange fees and receiving all exchange rebates. Such a policy would eliminate the agency problem with the broker, but it might not work if the broker uses order-routing procedures that the broker has optimized to minimize the net exchange fees that it pays on behalf of its clients. The goal for traders is not fee minimization but, rather, best execution.

Note that similar agency problems may also arise between the buy-side trading desk and the portfolio managers who use the desk if the desk does not pass through all fees and rebates to the beneficial accounts for which it trades.

At best, taker-maker pricing coupled with maker-taker pricing is a convoluted system for increasing price competition by providing more net pricing points. At worst, it facilitates quote-matching strategies; provides unfair advantages to HFTs, who best understand how the system works; and creates agency problems between brokers and their clients and possibly between buy-side desks and their portfolio managers.

## 6.8. Addressing Parasitic Trading Concerns

Some simple changes in market structure can protect slow traders from electronic parasitic traders. Here are some examples:

- Delayed trade reporting can frustrate the front running of buy-side algorithms. In particular, reporting trade prices as they occur but reporting aggregate sizes only after 10,000 shares have traded since the last report would greatly frustrate electronic traders who use machine-learning algorithms to detect large orders that buy-side algorithms break into smaller pieces.

- Larger minimum price variations (tick sizes) make quote matching expensive. A large tick forces traders to significantly improve prices when trading ahead. This conclusion assumes that exchange fee systems do not inadvertently create small tick sizes.

- Hidden orders are essential for protecting large buy-side traders from parasitic traders. Without such orders, traders hide the orders by not submitting them, which makes them hard to find and increases trading costs.

- Delayed processing of market orders can protect HFT liquidity suppliers from well-informed news traders who trade on the latest information distributed through electronic news feeds. Even a slight delay of only five milliseconds is enough to allow the HFTs to cancel their orders when news arrives. Allowing them to cancel their orders will reduce their losses to news traders, which will allow them to offer narrower spreads (better prices) to other traders. The effect on price efficiency would be trivial because information on electronic news feeds becomes common knowledge very quickly.

## 6.9. Special Order Types

Some electronic trading systems have created special order types that appeal to HFTs. These order types sometimes can disadvantage slower traders. For example, some exchanges support pegged limit orders that allow HFTs to continuously bid one tick below the best offer. These pegged orders adjust up and down as the best offer adjusts up and down. HFTs who want to continuously make market a tick below the best offer (usually in low-priced stocks) find these pegged orders useful because they do not have to cancel and replace their standing orders whenever the market moves.

Now consider the following situation: Suppose that an HFT is bidding at 19.99 with a floating limit order set at one tick below the current best offer of 20.00. Assume also that the market has additional size offered at 20.01. A large buyer submits a day limit order to buy at 20.00, with more size than is available in the market at 20.00—or possibly also below, for example, at the spread midpoint of 19.995. The buy order will immediately fill all available offered size at or below 20.00, the remainder will be posted in the book as the new bid at 20.00, the market will post a new best offer at 20.01, and the HFT's floating limit buy order will rise to 20.00.

Now, who should have precedence at the 20.00 bid? The large trader, whose order moved the market? Or the HFT, whose buy order was placed before the large trader's order? In principle, the exchange can set its rules as it pleases, subject to any regulatory oversight to which it may be subject. Potential problems arise, however, when the rules are not well known or, even more seriously, when they are not followed or when they are misrepresented to the public.

# 7. Conclusion and Final Comments

The single most important determinant of transaction costs is the decision to trade. Accordingly, transaction cost control cannot be separated from investment discipline. Traders who thoroughly understand why they and others trade will be more successful than those who do not.

Electronic markets and electronic trading have forever changed how people trade. The sell side has reacted and so too must the buy side. Although these new systems pose some regulatory problems, electronic markets are working well overall.

## 7.1. What about Bond Markets?

The electronic market structures of equity, futures, and options markets have attracted tremendous attention throughout the world. Much less attention has been given to the market structures of corporate and municipal bond markets, most of which, from the customer's point of view, have hardly changed since the late 19th century. Despite the efforts of many creative developers of electronic bond-trading systems, most public investors in these markets still trade largely over the counter with dealers.

The potential for electronic trading systems in these markets—and the attendant growth in electronic trading strategies—is quite large. Such systems undoubtedly will reflect the fact that bond issues—especially municipal bonds—vastly outnumber stock issues. Accordingly, except for the most actively traded bonds, limit order book trading systems will not be successful because buyers and sellers rarely will be present at the same time.

However, systems can be built that would allow public investors to trade with each other when both sides are present in the market. These systems would provide order display facilities where public investors and proprietary traders could post limit orders so that all traders could see them. If these facilities also had automatic execution mechanisms and if regulations or legal decisions prevent dealers from trading through displayed orders when arranging their own trades, bond transaction costs would drop substantially and bond trading would become much more active.

Many such electronic bond order-matching systems already exist, but they primarily serve dealers and not public investors. Recent empirical research suggests that public investors would greatly benefit if their brokers provided them with direct access to these systems as they presently do in the equity markets. Instead, most broker-dealers commonly interpose themselves

©2015 The CFA Institute Research Foundation. All Rights Reserved.

between their customers and these electronic markets. In transactions called riskless principal trades, these broker-dealers simultaneously buy on these electronic trading systems the bonds that they sell to their customers at substantial markups, and vice versa for customer sales. The markups play the role of brokerage commissions in these trades, but they generally are many times larger and, unlike commissions, broker-dealers do not disclose them to their customers. Bond investors seeking lower transaction costs should consider trading through those brokers who provide them with direct access to these innovative trading systems.

# Appendix A. The Flash Crash

The 6 May 2010 Flash Crash was the most notable market structure event in recent memory. During the crash, which started at about 2:42 p.m. ET, the E-mini S&P 500 futures contract dropped approximately 5% in 5 minutes and then recovered nearly fully in the next 10 minutes. The price volatility spilled from the equity futures market into the stock market, where some stocks traded down more than 99% or up more than 1,000%. In the immediate aftermath of the crash, regulators decided that more than 20,000 trades in more than 300 securities that occurred more than 60% away from earlier prices would be broken (canceled).

This extraordinary event raised many concerns about security market structure—in particular, how adoption of electronic trading may have increased potential systemic risks. This appendix describes the events that led up to the crash, what happened during the crash, and the regulatory responses to the crash.

## A.1. The Event and Its Causes

On Thursday, 6 May 2010, the stock market traded down throughout the day at an accelerating rate. By 2:30 p.m., it had lost about 4% from its previous close. Contemporaneous commentators attributed the fall to concerns about Greek sovereign debt and to the implications of a Greek default for other markets.

During the day, many traders who had been providing liquidity to the market were accumulating substantial long positions as people demanded to sell.[13] As the day wore on, their willingness to continue to accumulate additional inventory undoubtedly decreased. Moreover, day traders, who do not normally carry inventory overnight, were also considering how and when they would sell their losing positions.

Presumably in response to the European concerns and perhaps other concerns, portfolio managers at Waddell & Reed Financial Inc. (W&R) decided to reduce US equity exposure in their $27 billion Asset Strategy Fund by selling 75,000 June 2010 E-mini S&P 500 futures contracts worth approximately $4.1 billion. They gave this order to their buy-side trader, who proceeded to fill it using an algorithm that split the order into small pieces for execution. Although the order was the largest single order submitted to the E-mini futures market that year, it was not without precedent. Two earlier

---

[13]These traders did not include high-frequency dealers who generally maintained small inventories throughout the day, as is their normal practice.

orders in the previous year were of similar size or larger, one of which had been submitted by W&R. Those orders had been filled in more stable markets and over longer periods of time than W&R's 6 May order. The order started to execute at 2:32 p.m.

W&R's head trader, who normally would have handled such a large order, was out of the office that day. The order was handled by another trader in his office.

The trader set parameters on the algorithm to target an execution rate of 9% of the trading volume calculated over the previous minute without regard to price or time. This trading strategy was more aggressive than the one W&R had used to fill its large order from the previous year. The trader probably set an aggressive rate because he feared that the firm would obtain a worse execution if prices continued to fall. The more aggressive strategy contributed to the crash.

When the initial trades depressed S&P 500 futures prices, trading volumes increased substantially as arbitrageurs and others started to trade, many of them trading with each other as they normally did. The arbitrageurs bought the futures and sold equities and equity ETFs (exchange-traded funds), such as the SPDR S&P 500 ETF Trust (ticker SPY). Some arbitrageurs also sold call option contracts and bought put option contracts. The increase in trading volumes caused the algorithm to increase the rate of its order submissions as it tried to keep its mandate to participate in 9% of the market volume. The increasing order submission rate exacerbated the problem.

Initially, high-frequency traders and other liquidity suppliers in the E-mini futures markets supplied liquidity to W&R's order and accumulated long positions. Between 2:41 p.m. and 2:44 p.m., these short-term traders sold these positions as the algorithm continued to pump more orders into the market. During this four-minute period, the E-mini dropped 3%. By the end of this period, buy-side depth (total size of standing buy orders) in the E-mini contract dropped to only 1% of the average depth observed earlier in the day. The E-mini contract then dropped 1.7% in the next 15 seconds.

The arbitrage trades caused the equity markets to drop. In many securities—especially the ETFs—falling prices triggered stock loss market orders, which further depressed prices. The levered ETFs were particularly affected because their high volatilities make them popular with technical traders and retail traders, many of whom routinely place stop orders in an attempt to protect their positions.

As the prices changed quickly, many traders who were providing liquidity in the futures and equity markets dropped out, because they were unwilling to trade in the face of such extreme volatility. Many also had already accumulated large inventory positions from earlier in the day and did not want to buy more. Interestingly, researchers later discovered that the largest and most active high-frequency-trading firms did not withdraw. Nonetheless, limit order books thinned out—especially on the buy side—as traders canceled standing orders and as sellers filled those buy orders still standing.

In some stocks, all standing buy orders were exhausted and trading stopped. In other stocks, all buy orders except those placed with a limit price of only a penny or two were exhausted. In these stocks, exchange trading systems blindly filled market sell orders at extraordinarily low prices. In a few other stocks, the withdrawal of liquidity suppliers from the market also removed essentially all liquidity from the sell side of the market. Some stocks then traded at prices as high as $100,000 when market buy orders were filled against sell orders placed at extraordinarily high prices.

The slide stopped at 2:45:28 p.m., when a Chicago Mercantile Exchange trading rule called Stop Logic Functionality caused the exchange's computers to briefly halt trading in the E-mini S&P 500 futures contract and to clear the limit order book of all standing limit orders. The rule is triggered when it becomes apparent that pending order executions would cause prices to jump too far. The futures contract dropped about 5% from when the algorithm started to trade at 2:32 p.m. to the market halt at 2:45 p.m. The algorithm sold about 35,000 contracts during this period.

When trading resumed five seconds later, the buy-side algorithm continued to trade, but many liquidity suppliers were now willing to provide liquidity. Prices rose quickly in orderly markets.

The episode largely ended when the big W&R order completed filling at around 2:51 p.m., about 20 minutes after it started. However, the market remained quite volatile during the remainder of the day as traders adjusted their positions and responded to the extreme volatility.

Following the crash, regulators broke all trades that had occurred more than 60% away from the previous close.

## A.2. Implications for Traders

The Flash Crash provided three important lessons for observant traders. First, market orders are incompatible with electronic order-matching systems that do not curb trading when prices move too quickly. Had traders priced all their orders, no trades would have taken place at unreasonably high or low prices. Following the crash, many retail brokers adopted a policy of converting all customer market orders into marketable limit orders with limit prices set about 10% above the current ask for buy orders and 10% below the current bid for sell orders.

Second, institutional traders using algorithms need to be very careful not to demand more liquidity than orderly markets can provide. Most buy-side investors probably immediately recognized that W&R lost a substantial amount of its clients' money owing to the extraordinarily high transaction costs associated with the trade. To obtain a crude estimate of this loss, assume that the algorithm traded all $4.1 billion of its order at a uniform rate throughout the 5% price reversal. The average market impact of the trade would have been 2.5%, which implies total transaction costs of about $100 million, or 0.37% of the $27 billion in assets of the W&R Asset Strategy Fund. Such significant losses attract attention. Within a week, many algorithm writers probably coded limits into their algorithms to help prevent them from being used irresponsibly.

Finally, algorithm writers and the traders who use algorithms must pay much more attention to the dangers of using algorithms that can create destructive feedback loops. In particular, they need to be much more careful about understanding how algorithms respond to market conditions that they may create themselves.

## A.3.  Regulatory Responses

Following the Flash Crash, regulators adopted new rules to prevent a similar crash from happening again. They placed curbs that halt trades in a stock for five minutes if prices move up or down by more than 10% for large stocks and 20% for smaller stocks. This rule ensures that prices cannot move too quickly, but it does not prevent traders from behaving foolishly. Had it been in effect during the Flash Crash, the rule would have stopped trades from occurring at ridiculously low or high prices, but it would not have stopped the W&R trader from submitting an unrealistically aggressive order.

Regulators also adopted rules to establish when and which trades will be broken in the event of another extreme price change. Such rules should help ensure that liquidity suppliers who are afraid that their trades may be broken do not withdraw from the market prematurely.

# RESEARCH FOUNDATION
# CONTRIBUTION FORM

☑ **Yes**, I want the Research Foundation to continue to fund innovative research that advances the investment management profession. Please accept my tax-deductible contribution at the following level:

Thought Leadership Circle................ US$1,000,000 or more
Named Endowment...................... US$100,000 to US$999,999
Research Fellow ........................... US$10,000 to US$99,999
Contributing Donor........................ US$1,000 to US$9,999
Friend ............................................. Up to US$999

I would like to donate $ _____ .

☐ My check is enclosed (payable to the CFA Institute Research Foundation).
☐ I would like to donate appreciated securities (send me information).
☐ Please charge my donation to my credit card.
      ■ VISA  ■ MC  ■ Amex  ■ Diners

| | | | | | | | | | | | | | | | | |
|---|---|---|---|---|---|---|---|---|---|---|---|---|---|---|---|---|---|

Card Number

___/___                    _____
Expiration Date           Name on card   P L E A S E   P R I N T
☐ Corporate Card
☐ Personal Card          _____
                              Signature
☐ This is a pledge. Please bill me for my donation of $ _____
☐ I would like recognition of my donation to be:
      ■ Individual donation  ■ Corporate donation  ■ Different individual

_____
PLEASE PRINT NAME OR COMPANY NAME AS YOU WOULD LIKE IT TO APPEAR

PLEASE PRINT   ☐ Mr. ☐ Mrs. ☐ Ms.   MEMBER NUMBER _____

_____
Last Name (Family Name)          First          Middle Initial

_____
Title

_____
Address

_____
City                    State/Province        Country ZIP/Postal Code

**Please mail this completed form with your contribution to:**
**The CFA Institute Research Foundation • P.O. Box 2082**
**Charlottesville, VA 22902-2082 USA**

For more on the CFA Institute Research Foundation, please visit
www.cfainstitute.org/learning/foundation/Pages/index.aspx.